THE ANNUAL CAMPAIGN

Kelly —

Thanks for all that
you are doing to grow
Philanthropy at the Y!

Erik D. Anderson

THE ANNUAL CAMPAIGN

Erik J. Daubert, MBA, ACFRE

WILEY

John Wiley & Sons, Inc.

For general information on our other products and services, or technical support, please contact our Customer Care Department within the United States at 800-762-2974, outside the United States at 317-572-3993 or fax 317-572-4002.

Wiley also publishes its books in a variety of electronic formats. Some content that appears in print may not be available in electronic books.

For more information about Wiley products, visit our Web site at http://www.wiley.com.

ISBN: 978–0–470–43863–3

Printed in the United States of America.

10 9 8 7 6 5 4 3 2 1

The AFP Fund Development Series

The AFP Fund Development Series is intended to provide fund development professionals and volunteers, including board members (and others interested in the nonprofit sector), with top-quality publications that help advance philanthropy as voluntary action for the public good. Our goal is to provide practical, timely guidance and information on fundraising, charitable giving, and related subjects. The Association of Fundraising Professionals (AFP) and Wiley each bring to this innovative collaboration unique and important resources that result in a whole greater than the sum of its parts. For information on other books in the series, please visit:

www.afpnet.org

The Association of Fundraising Professionals

The Association of Fundraising Professionals (AFP) represents over 30,000 members in more than 197 chapters throughout the United States, Canada,

Mexico, and China, working to advance philanthropy through advocacy, research, education, and certification programs.

The association fosters development and growth of fundraising professionals and promotes high ethical standards in the fundraising profession. For more information or to join the world's largest association of fundraising professionals, visit www.afpnet.org.

2008-2009 AFP Publishing Advisory Committee

Chair: Nina P. Berkheiser, CFRE
Principal Consultant, Your Nonprofit Advisor

Linda L. Chew, CFRE
Development Consultant

D. C. Dreger, ACFRE
Senior Campaign Director, Custom Development Solutions, Inc. (CDS)

Patricia L. Eldred, CFRE
Director of Development, Independent Living Inc.

Samuel N. Gough, CFRE
Principal, The AFRAM Group

Audrey P. Kintzi, ACFRE
Director of Development, Courage Center

Steven Miller, CFRE
Director of Development and Membership, Bread for the World

Robert J. Mueller, CFRE
Vice President, Hospice Foundation of Louisville

Maria Elena Noriega
Director, Noriega Malo & Associates

Michele Pearce
Director of Development, Consumer Credit Counseling Service of Greater Atlanta

Leslie E. Weir, MA, ACFRE

Director of Family Philanthropy, The Winnipeg Foundation

Sharon R. Will, CFRE

Director of Development, South Wind Hospice

John Wiley & Sons, Inc.:

Susan McDermott

Senior Editor (Professional / Trade Division)

AFP Staff:

Jan Alfieri

Manager, New Product Development

Rhonda Starr

Vice President, Education and Training

This book is dedicated to all the people who have ever toiled in the efforts of ethically raising money for nonprofit organizations. While it is not easy work, it makes our world a much better place.

Contents

Preface

This book shows nonprofit professionals and volunteers how to run the human efforts of an annual support campaign. There are great books on direct mail, telephone soliciting, Internet fundraising at your nonprofit organization, and so many other fundraising topics.

This book is not one of those.

My goal is to explain how to run a high-functioning annual support campaign with volunteers and staff acting as partners. I strive to impart basic knowledge as well as best practice solutions for people in any stage of their fundraising career. For people who may be new to this subject, I outline how to set up and manage an annual support campaign and its many components. I attempt to lay out as much as possible about the annual campaign—from what a campaign should look like in design, to how to recruit and engage volunteers in the integral work of annual campaign friend raising and fundraising. For those with annual support campaign experience, I bring attention to areas that are important to focus on to make your efforts more effective with greater results. For those with less than successful annual support campaign attempts in their past, take heart: This book works to give you solid ideas for how to make an annual support campaign that will be more successful. As well, there are exercises throughout the text; be bold and jot down your ideas in the book as you go along. At the end, you will come away with a tremendous head start for making your annual campaign great.

Chapter 1 outlines the many components of the overall annual fund, which is the 12-month fundraising efforts of a nonprofit organization to raise money for yearly operational needs. This information begins to reveal how the annual support campaign fits into yearly fundraising as a whole at your organization and what a foundational piece it can be if done well.

Chapter 2 then makes the case that the annual campaign should be the cornerstone for your annual fund program and begins to establish some basic concepts. Well-run and high-functioning annual support campaigns are almost always the most effective means for raising money and for sharing the story of the important work that you do each and every day, month and year at your nonprofit.

Chapter 3 discusses the issues that you may face in determining how ready you are to embark on the annual support campaign program. It includes many aspects of nonprofit financial development management and encourages you to analyze each one prior to beginning your annual support campaign. Far from being discouraging, it is meant to show things that you should consider prior to beginning annual support at your nonprofit. Note that the assumption is that you will begin!

Chapter 4 discusses how and why to develop a strong case for support regarding your annual support campaign. How do you write and create a strong case? What needs to be included? What are the most impactful aspects of your nonprofit? This chapter includes these and other features regarding your story and how to tell it to your community.

Chapter 5 shows you how to recruit and establish a volunteer workforce in your annual support campaign. It illuminates how integral volunteers are to the overall success of your campaign and the need to take care to engage them purposefully. Volunteers are a source of much energy for your organization and need to be appreciated and maintained.

Chapter 6 illustrates why and how you should design campaign teams to tell the story of your organization and to raise money for your charitable mission. The staff, board, major gifts and community gifts teams all play a special part in the entire effort that is the annual support campaign.

Chapter 7 discusses how relationships are a foundational piece of a nonprofit's ultimate success. We then review procedures and tips regarding the "ask" for money from donors and prospective donors. With details on how to understand your donors and then ultimately ask them for gifts and pledges, it is an invaluable resource for those interested in maximizing charitable funds.

Chapter 8 helps you to figure out where you are and where you want to go. It also contains a timeline for keeping your annual support campaign on track and organized. Attention is given to how good planning will serve you well and evaluations will help you learn more with each campaign.

The goal of this text is to show you methods and explain the rationale behind certain strategies. You will come away with the necessary tools to run a highly effective annual support campaign that will raise more money annually and position your nonprofit organization to thrive in future fundraising endeavors. Whether your organization is approaching its first annual support campaign or its hundredth, you are sure to find helpful tips, hints, stories, and techniques within these pages.

Best wishes for a great annual support campaign experience!

Erik J. Daubert MBA, ACFRE

Acknowledgments

I am so thankful to my wife and first line editor, Andrea, who helped shape not only the words of this text but also the flow and general content. Without her, this book would be much less than it is.

I am also thankful to AFP and John Wiley & Sons for approaching me and giving me the opportunity to write *The Annual Campaign*. It has been a privilege to work with everyone involved in the publishing of this book.

A book of this type does not come together without the decades of working with many talented individuals. I have been fortunate to have in my fundraising experience some great teachers and mentors including but not limited to: James Greenfield, Judy Bright, Shannon Williams, Ceil Weatherman, Jim Epps, and all members of the YMCA of the USA Consulting Team, with special thanks to Steve Burns, Mike Bussey, Doug Goodfellow, Carol Schmidt, Gerry Hundt, and Courtney Weiland. My gratitude extends to so many great staff and volunteers including but not limited to: Doug McMillan, Lacy Presnell, John Alexander, Jr., Eliza Kraft Olander, Kay Morgan, Jim Stewart, and Bill Malloy to name a few. Thanks also to The Akiba School of Dallas, Texas, The Evelina Children's Hospital of London, England, and the University of California—Irvine for allowing their case statement documents to be shared with readers as examples in this book. I am also thankful to the many educational institutions that have been foundational cornerstones of my learning in fundraising and so many other areas. I am appreciative of all the people at the many diverse nonprofit organizations who I have had as clients over my years of fundraising. I am equally as thankful to the many students I have taught from all over the world, as they each have allowed me to gain wisdom and insight as we worked to strengthen their unique programs and improve their communities. Particular thanks is due to the YMCA movement, as I have worked with so many fabulous YMCAs over the years. The YMCA of the USA and the YMCA of the Triangle Area were particularly helpful in so much of my philanthropic training and experience and also in the creation of this book. It has been an honor and a privilege to be involved with the largest nonprofit in the United States for so many years.

I am also grateful to my friends and family who have remained with me over the course of this great journey. My mother and father, Bob and Madeline Daubert, my sister, Lisa, and my brother, David, have all helped to make me the person I am today.

Thank you to everyone involved, both mentioned and unmentioned. I appreciate you!

About the Author

With almost two decades of nonprofit experience, Erik Daubert is regarded as a leader in the areas of development and nonprofit management. In addition to a broad-based career in nonprofits, he has served as a consultant and founding partner of a consulting firm. Erik formerly served as Association Financial Development Consultant for the YMCA of the USA, serving YMCA associations across the United States.

Erik's education includes degrees and certificates from the University of North Carolina at Chapel Hill, Duke University, Stanford University, Indiana University, Campbell University, and the National Outdoor Leadership School (NOLS). He is an Association of Fundraising Professionals Master Trainer and has served as an instructor for the Duke University Program in Non-Profit Management, the North American YMCA Development Organization, AFP, and the YMCA of the USA, among others. He has delivered trainings for nonprofit professionals across North America and holds the title of Advanced Certified Fund Raising Executive, as recognized by the Association of Fundraising Professionals; he is the 81st individual worldwide to have obtained this lifetime credential. Erik volunteers with and has worked with a variety of nonprofits, and brings with him a unique combination of nonprofit fundraising and board understanding. He has worked directly with a variety of nonprofit organizations primarily in the United States.

Erik has been personally involved in the raising of millions and millions of dollars, which has included work in annual, endowment, and capital campaigns.

He has been recognized nationally or locally by these organizations:

Child Advocacy Commission

Coca-Cola

Eno River Association

International Who's Who

National Arbor Day Foundation

North American YMCA Development Organization

Nourish International

Olympic Games

Public Allies North Carolina

Sierra Club

Stanford University—Center for Social Innovation

Triangle Business Journal

Triangle United Way

Who's Who in America

YMCA of the USA

Erik lives in Durham, North Carolina with his wife, Andrea, and his cat, Jasper.

THE ANNUAL
CAMPAIGN

## CHAPTER 1

What Is the Annual Fund?

After reading this chapter, you will be able to:

- Understand the various components of the annual fund program.
- Begin to see that the annual support campaign is a foundational piece of the overall financial development effort.
- Describe possible annual fund options for your nonprofit organization.
- List the various aspects of your overall annual fund program.

Before we begin to discuss the annual campaign specifically, it is helpful to understand the context of the overall annual fund within a nonprofit organization. In order to do this effectively, we must first understand the components of a typical annual fund.

The components of the annual fund usually include the annual support campaign, grants, special events, Internet fundraising, federated campaign efforts such as the United Way or Earth Share, direct mail, individual appeals, telephone fundraising, and corporate appeals. While additional components are discussed at the end of this chapter, the components just mentioned often make up the entire annual fund for most nonprofit organizations. Each of these components also has importance in the overall organizational financial development plan.

Annual Campaign

A well-run annual support campaign is the cornerstone of most great annual fund programs. Performed properly, the annual support campaign is not only the most valuable public relations and marketing tools that an organization has; it also is one of the most highly effective ways of raising contributed support. Well-run annual support campaign teams thoughtfully utilize volunteers to engage prospects and donors in the philanthropic process. An effective annual support campaign has four components: staff, board, major gifts, and community gifts. By engaging staff, board, volunteers, donors, and prospects in the philanthropic process of the annual support campaign, you help to ensure that your organization will raise the most money possible with the best possible return on investment. Volunteer-driven annual support campaigns represent one of the most lucrative returns on investment of any nonprofit activity. It is quite common for fundraising costs of well-run annual support campaigns to be only 8% to 12% of the overall annual support campaign goal. This shows that annual support campaigns are worthwhile and effective methods of raising funds for the smallest nonprofit organization or the largest. Compared to other methods of fundraising, annual support campaigns can be a highly efficient way of raising contributed income. More details on this integral cornerstone of your financial development program are given throughout the book.

Grants

Every day nonprofits around the world receive grants from entities ranging from the federal government to the smallest of family foundations. Every new financial development professional's dream seems to be identifying a project and then writing a huge grant to fund it in its entirety. In reality, getting grants is far more laborious than it would first appear. Additionally, grants tend to be less reliable as a long term funding stream for nonprofit organizations. While foundations theoretically exist just to give away money, the demands on their time and treasure are usually very high. Foundations often want to fund new and exciting projects; typically they are not excited about sustaining long-term funding to any particular organization. This makes operational grant getting for annual programs and projects challenging.

Grants typically come from one of these sources:

- Government
- Corporate foundations
- Private foundations
- Family foundations
- Community foundations

Depending on the funder that you approach, you can get grants for different projects, programs, or purposes. Although this text is not focused on grants specifically, it may be helpful for you to know and understand that foundations boards are just groups of people brought together around a foundation's purpose. My point in stating this is to highlight that foundation boards are just people like you and me. Approach them with the respect and cultivation process that you would approach any donor, and likely you will meet with a much higher chance of success.

Often you can research foundations that are of interest to you at your local public library. You can also learn a great deal about foundations and their interests through the Foundation Center and its resource collections. For more information about the Foundation Center and its resources, go to http:// fdncenter.org.

In the context of the annual fund, I encourage you to track grants separately from your annual campaign and other fundraising efforts. Each of the annual fund components that your organization has should have its own focus, budget, time, and attention.

IN THE REAL WORLD

Live and Learn

In one of my early development positions, my chief executive officer (CEO) asked me to meet with him and a local foundation board member. The meeting was to be about the possibility of the foundation providing us with a grant for a key program.

The mission of the foundation had virtually nothing to do with our program area, and I told my CEO that I firmly believed that he was wasting his time and mine. The foundation's mission simply did not align with our key objectives. He asked me to humor him and give my best efforts to the meeting. We prepared fully and scheduled the appointment with the foundation board member. What I was unaware of was this individual's deep and long-standing relationship with our organization.

After the meeting and appropriate proposal submission, we were given a fairly large grant for our program. The board member had been impressed with our service to the community and with our program offering.

I learned two huge lessons at this meeting:

1 Foundations can support programs of interest whether they align with their stated purpose or not.

2 Having strong relationships with foundation board members can make great things happen for your nonprofit organization, regardless of the mission of the foundation.

TIPS AND TECHNIQUES

Tips to Remember When Submitting a Grant Proposal

Have you:

- Directly contacted the foundation via telephone, well written introductory letter or personal visit?

- Checked to see who else in your community might be making a similar request or doing similar work?

(continued)

- Involved the foundation board or key foundation staff in actually planning and structuring your proposal?
- Followed the grant request presentation format and guidelines exactly as outlined?
- Outlined the community challenge and your organizational solution without using acronyms that may be unclear to the reader?
- Considered collaborations with other agencies as a possible solution to a community need or challenge?
- Taken the time to make sure that your proposal is well written and grammatically correct?
- Made the foundation deadline for submission and review?
- Focused on what makes your grant request special or unique from other requests that they may receive?
- Developed a plan on how you will evaluate the success or failure of your efforts once you receive a grant?
- Described your organization in terms that adequately tell of your mission and purpose?
- Sent all appropriate copies and signatures?
- Made sure that key individuals (such as your CEO, chief volunteer officer, and key foundation contacts) know that you are submitting your proposal?

Grants can play a valuable part in a financial development program, yet relying on them solely as a funding source can lead to very hard times over the course of an organization's life. A well-run annual support campaign can keep you from depending too heavily on grants as a funding source.

Special Events

I believe that fundraising special events, especially at smaller nonprofit organizations, are one of the most overused and overestimated forms of fundraising used in America today. You can certainly raise money through special events, but often there are easier and more effective ways. Still, special events are great for building awareness about your nonprofit mission and about your organization's efforts in your community. Special events can also help generate publicity, visibility, and awareness for a nonprofit mission that might otherwise not receive a lot of attention. Special events can even provide venues to recognize key volunteers, programs, or staff members when utilized strategically.

TIPS AND TECHNIQUES

Ten Reasons to Do Special Events

Special events can:

❶ Be energizing and fun.

❷ Create needed funding for immediate use.

❸ Increase an organization's visibility in the community and improve its image.

❹ Be another opportunity for donors to give to and support your organization.

❺ Be an occasion to identify and cultivate new donors.

❻ Be another chance to promote the organization's mission.

❼ Be used as a focal point for showcasing key programs or services.

❽ Be a great time to honor and recognize people important to the organization.

❾ Be a chance to create volunteer participation around an uplifting and motivating experience.

❿ Be a good arena to highlight corporate sponsorship opportunities and create venues for corporate sponsor exposure.

Special events range widely and are as creative and diverse as the people and organizations that sponsor them. There is virtually no limit to the ideas and themes that can be utilized in an effort to raise visibility and funding for needy organizations.

Special events represent opportunities for people to become involved with your organization who might not otherwise join in assisting you with your important mission work. Often people are attracted by the special event itself rather than by the organization's mission. The key with special events is to get people interested in your organization while they are at the special event. Remember that after you introduce people to your organization through this special event, you need to create a way to somehow follow-up with them and ultimately to show them an even more meaningful way to get involved.

TIPS AND TECHNIQUES

Some Things to Think about Before the Event

- What is the best location for this event?
- How should we price this event?
- How many people are expected?
- How much should we budget to spend per person?
- Have we contacted the local or appropriate media as appropriate?
- How can we make sure that people have a great time?
- What will we need to purchase or rent in order to hold this event?
- What should we do in case of inclement weather?

In my experience, people very much underestimate the real costs of special events and overestimate the amount of actual money raised. Most special events take an inordinate amount of staff and volunteer time with minimal return on investment. I often challenge organizations to consider whether the event is truly a fundraiser or whether it is better utilized as a donor cultivation or marketing and communications event. Nonprofit organizations often call these events "friendraisers" as they are more about making friends than raising funding. Many events may be worth doing for publicity or visibility purposes but are not effective fundraisers. Also, do not be afraid to stop doing a specific event; just because you have been doing an event for a long period of time does not mean that you have to do it again this year.

Almost always, the biggest benefit of a special event is not in the money raised but in the awareness and goodwill generated by it. Ideally, people in your community who have never heard of your organization prior to the event become aware of it through their special event participation. Then they become involved in your organization, ultimately becoming more meaningfully connected over time.

Creative Ways to Build Your Prospect Lists around Special Events

- Use your own lists and directories to identify people who might want to be invited to your event. Ask these individuals to bring additional friends and colleagues who might be interested in learning more about your organization.
- Call your key contacts, and ask them to bring people who might be able to move your organization forward through their involvement.
- Consider giving complimentary tickets (as appropriate) to key individuals as thank-yous for previous efforts as well as to encourage attendance.
- Consider inviting key public relations personnel from major companies in your area.
- Publish and promote your event in your newsletter and email notifications.
- Promote your event through the local media. Take advantage of community calendars and other venues to publicize your event as widely as possible.
- Attend networking meetings that make sense for your type of organization. Focus on getting business cards and contact information from others, and follow up after the meeting.
- Promote your efforts on your Web site. Keep your Web site as up to date as possible, discussing the event beforehand and reporting back on it after it has occurred.
- Post your upcoming event on message boards as appropriate.
- Consider writing blogs or other web articles about your upcoming function.
- Review what companies sponsor events like yours in the community to see if they would be interested in sponsoring your function.
- To get information on all guests who attend your event, hold a drawing at the event that people sign up to participate in or have a sign-in sheet at the door.

(continued)

- Consider offering prizes for people who connect your organization the most to others in the community. Who brought the most people? Who sold the most tickets?
- Consider asking and encouraging participation from local politicians at your special event.

Building prospect lists from special events can help strengthen your other fundraising efforts. Remember that the main goal of special events is to bring people closer to your organization. As mentioned, special events are rarely the best method to fundraise. As with any component of your financial development plan, keeping your special event focused by having clear objectives, will help it to be most successful.

 TIPS AND TECHNIQUES

Some Things to Do after the Special Event

- Thank people for coming and let them know how their participation made and could make a difference.
- Call key people to let them know how much their help was appreciated.
- Write key individuals to thank them for their efforts in hosting and holding the event.
- Report back to donors, corporate sponsors, and participants about how much money was raised and how it will be used to help advance your mission.
- Have a follow-up meeting to evaluate what worked well and what could have gone better so that you can learn from your successes and your failures.
- Write an article and include a picture of the event in your organizational newsletter.
- Consider sending an article with a photograph to your local newspaper.
- Post updated photos and information about the event on your website, blogs or other appropriate electronic media.

(continued)

(*continued*)

- Thank your event committees and consider honoring key individuals and supporters as appropriate at a board meeting or other event.
- Consider thank-you gifts if appropriate for key people and sponsors. These do not have to be expensive. Personal is almost always the best answer.
- Decide if the event is worth doing again next year. If the event has not been successful, consider stopping it or modifying it.
- Review the budget and all expenses to see where you could or should have improved.
- Prepare the next year's planning calendar.

Most of these things should be done within one week after the event. Timely wrap-up is important for several reasons:

- You capture the most from the review process while it is still fresh in people's minds.
- Employees have not moved on to other things and are too busy to finish up these details.
- You capitalize on the momentum from the event to engage your new constituents.
- Thank-yous are best when timely.

Well-run special events can help build your donor list, raise money, get media coverage, and get to know volunteers and donors in addition to, it is hoped, implementing your mission through the event itself. Remember, however, that special events can be extremely time-consuming and typically are not a highly recommended focal strategy for annual fund efforts. The well-run annual support campaign typically raises far more funds far more effectively than special events.

 IN THE REAL WORLD

One of my first positions in development was as director of marketing and special events, and one of my first professional responsibilities was to plan

(*continued*)

and implement our annual fundraising auction. Working with a committee of dedicated and committed volunteers and staff, we planned a sock hop auction/dinner/dance. Part of my job was to secure the donations necessary to hold the event in our local gymnasium.

I worked tirelessly for the months leading up to the event itself and managed to get a ton of donated food items, auction items, and other goodies in an effort to make the auction one of our most successful ever. It was; it raised approximately $9,000 for the charity. That may not seem like much, but the organization had a very small operating budget, so this was considered a big success.

The problem was that I knew how much time and effort all of us had put into the event. I knew that it had not actually raised anything at all when one accounted for my salary, the volunteer time, the gas and other expenses collecting all of the auction items, and all of the other variables that went into hosting and implementing this event. The next year we stopped doing this auction and put our efforts into our first annual support campaign. We raised more than $50,000 on the annual campaign and did a much better job of telling our story in the community—all while raising our image and status as a nonprofit mission-based organization. A much better return on our investment!

Federated Campaigns

A federated campaign is a fundraising program that is run by a non-profit organization that then distributes the funds to other nonprofit agencies. Federated campaigns such as United Way, Earth Share, Combined Federal Campaigns, State Employees Campaign, and others play an important role in America's philanthropic process. Workplace giving campaigns can be very enthusiastic, and employers across the United States utilize these campaigns to raise the community awareness of charitable organizations in many positive ways. As of this writing, the United Way of America remains the top charity organization in the United States in terms of raising contributed dollars. Federated efforts can be highly effective ways to raise money for charitable organizations that fit within their funding parameters. Federated efforts can also allow nonprofit organizations to gain access to the hearts and minds of some of the most influential and affluent companies in your region. The challenge with relying on these entities as a sole source of funding, however, is in your individual organization's long-term sustainability and in making sure that your organization gets the community time and attention that it deserves. When these federated campaigns do well, there is more money for everyone involved. When these federated campaigns do poorly, however, every nonprofit organization suffers as well. If your organization is to be truly self-reliant, it is critical that you develop and strengthen your own financial development programs. A well-run annual support campaign is a great way to build awareness about your organization and raise dollars through contributed support.

Advertising

While there are exceptions to every rule, advertising usually does not generate a substantial result in generating from donors much of a philanthropic response. There are simply too many charities and too many good causes for people to be motivated to give by a billboard or a newspaper advertisement. Think about the last time that you were driving down the road and saw a billboard for a good cause. Did you stop, pull over, grab your cellular telephone, and call in a pledge? Probably not. While advertising and promotional information about your worthy cause may help you to build your brand or generate positive feelings, rarely will advertising alone generate any actual response.

In the case of universities, advertising the campaign or other philanthropic efforts in alumni publications and newsletters is a positive way to educate and develop the constituency for philanthropy. But again, typically it does not produce fantastic direct results.

The exceptions to this rule usually concern very public disasters or other unique occurrences in our society. Advertising can have tremendous impact after national and international disasters. On the effectiveness scale of the annual fund, however, advertising usually ranks very low when compared to the annual support campaign.

Commemorative Giving

Nonprofit agencies often promote or create opportunities for individuals to commemorate the life or death of a loved one or a respected member of the community. Some agencies place these funds into their endowment to fund future programming; others put these funds into the annual fund. Because commemorative giving is often a one-time occurrence, I typically recommend placing these dollars into the endowment of an organization. Some nonprofit agencies, particularly young, less established organizations, utilize these funds in the year that they are generated for annual fund purposes.

Commercial Sales Concepts

There exists an almost countless variety of ways to utilize commercial sales opportunities as a part of the overall annual fund. A couple of examples include:

- Marketing any number of products or services to create revenue streams that support the nonprofit organization.
- Collaboration between for-profit and nonprofit, as when a company, such as a cereal company, gives a certain amount of sales for each product unit sold.
- Collaboration between a credit card company and a nonprofit. Sometimes MasterCard or Visa allows for a percentage of the purchases utilized on a card to be donated to charity. Credit cards can also be a part of an organization's marketing and awareness efforts.

These types of arrangements are unlikely to generate enough revenue to support the organization effectively but may act as an additional income stream for some organizations. Although these sources offer some opportunity to generate funds, the money raised is usually related to purchases by a consumer and are considered to be less philanthropic.

Games of Chance

Nonprofit organizations sometimes become involved with any number of gambling efforts or games of chance. These include casino nights, bingo, charity game tickets, keno, raffles, frog races, cockroach races, and everything in between. I do not encourage these types of efforts in my consulting work as they seem to encourage gaming more than philanthropy. Some organizations have found these to be successful and fun events for their constituencies although others have had issues with permitting and the local government. Before embarking on any charity effort associated with a game of chance, make sure to look closely and fully understand the laws associated with such efforts.

Door-to-Door and Street Solicitation

The challenge with door-to-door solicitation is that it is a truly random method of fundraising. It also takes a large amount of human resource effort to accomplish. Additionally, it typically leads only to smaller gifts as people are generally reluctant to give large amounts of money or intrinsically personal information to someone whom they seem to meet by chance. Recently, however, street solicitations have taken on new life, especially in major cities, where there has been some success with subscription-type sign-ups. This is where someone approaches you representing a charity and encourages a gift of $X per month to help save a child or adopt a wild animal or the like. Large recognizable organizations are likely to have much greater success with this type of effort than smaller and more obscure nonprofits with less name recognition.

Mass Media

In this context, "mass media" is related to fundraising efforts such as infomercials and televangelism type shows. If you think about the last time you saw a religious evangelist on television who was also raising money for their church, you will get one image of a multimedia fundraising effort.

Another example is infomercials that have often been citing children's or other poverty issues in developing countries. These expensive multimedia efforts use television as a powerful medium to share and state their case for support as well as to portray the need of their constituency, whether as saved children or saved souls. While these can be successful in raising funds and building larger constituencies, most nonprofit organizations do not have the resources necessary to undertake such ventures.

Telethons and Radiothons

If you have ever watched television over Labor Day weekend in the United States, you may have seen a dramatic example of a telethon with the Jerry Lewis Labor Day Muscular Dystrophy Telethon. This strategy is also widely used by the Corporation for Public Broadcasting. The ability to take over the airwaves of a station or stations to espouse your cause and story can be a broad reaching method for spreading the story about the fundraising needs and concerns of a nonprofit organization.

IN THE REAL WORLD

I worked with a nonprofit in the rural western part of the United States that used a radiothon as part of its public phase efforts to finish up a large campaign project. The nonprofit was in a small town that served as a hub for a broadly dispersed community that utilized it as the community center. Because of the geographical challenges associated with being in an extremely rural environment, the radiothon enabled the nonprofit to convey and explain their efforts to a larger audience than it would have been able to without a broader media effort. It was highly successful in raising more than $250,000. This strategy is being used more and more by local hospitals and other nonprofits to tell the story of children's issues and medical concerns as well as to generate philanthropic funds to serve the local community. Such efforts, however, can be difficult for most nonprofits to organize and implement due to the resources that must be mobilized.

E-mail and Instant Messaging

As technology changes and advances, there is an increased use of email, instant messaging, texting, and other electronic communications for education and solicitation. In my mind, these represent a hybrid extension of the direct mail concept (personal letter) and the telephone solicitation. In some ways, these concepts bring the urgency of a telephone call to the written message of a personal note or letter. An electronic message can convey a timeliness and immediacy that a phone call traditionally has taken and also may be more readily read and accepted than a telephone call. These efforts are becoming more and more commonplace as a method of donor and prospect communication. These tools can be highly effective methods for fundraising—if they are utilized properly and as part of an overall fundraising strategy. E-mail and instant messaging are discussed later in this text in the community gifts section of the annual support campaign.

While each of the additional sources of annual fund revenue listed have merit, the best method of annual operational fundraising for most nonprofit organizations remains the annual support campaign. The remainder of this text focuses on this preeminent method and model for generating annual fundraising and philanthropic support.

Summary

The annual fund is made up of many different components depending on the nonprofit organization, its level of maturity, and the other fundraising efforts it has under way. Many nonprofit organizations utilize a highly diverse group of fundraising strategies to raise the funds needed to sustain their missions on an annual basis. These may include everything from credit cards to games of chance to participation in federated campaign efforts like United Way.

There are many different ways to raise additional contributed support on an annual basis. Although these methods can generate valuable dollars for some organizations, I contend that for most nonprofit organizations, the annual support campaign remains the best way to tell the story of your organization and raise contributed funds. Whatever efforts a nonprofit undertakes to raise charitable funds on an annual basis, the annual campaign should be a foundational component of the annual fund. Track and monitor the various fundraising methods of the annual fund such as grants, special events and raffles independently and separately from the annual support campaign in order to adequately monitor and evaluate each method. Evaluating each unit of your annual fund effort separately will allow you to assess each component's effectiveness on a case by case basis. This will allow you continue to do those that generate the most positive returns and ultimately create a better short- and long-term fundraising program.

## CHAPTER 2

Benefits of the Annual Campaign

After reading this chapter, you will be able to:

- Understand the benefits of the annual support campaign in your overall fundraising efforts.
- Realize the multitude of rewards of an annual support campaign program.
- Acknowledge the widespread benefits for staff members, volunteers and the larger community, by having a well-run annual support campaign.

The annual support campaign serves a variety of roles for the nonprofit organization. The annual campaign is about raising awareness, engaging volunteers, getting your organizational message out into the broader community, and yes, even raising money. It is an extremely powerful part of a financial development program and can be the cornerstone of overall philanthropic support to your nonprofit.

Before we begin to examine the many functions of the annual support campaign in your organization, it is worth taking a moment to understand where donors give their gifts. As nonprofits, we survive or thrive on donors giving their gifts to our organizations in support of our missions and efforts in the community. So, where do donors give their gifts?

Where Do Donors Give?

Organizations that Meet Critical Needs in the Community

Regardless of the size or scope of your organization, donors want to know that their money is being used to meet an important need in the community. Whether your community is made up of the entire world or just a small portion of it, your donors want to know that their money will be used to meet critical needs. One of your first responsibilities as a development professional is to understand and be able to synthesize these needs. It is absolutely essential that you fully understand what it is that your organization is trying to accomplish and why the need for charitable funds exists. It is only after you truly assimilate this information that you will be able to extol your organization's needs in a way that the community will easily comprehend and support.

Organizations that They Respect

Donors also want to give to agencies and organizations that they respect and in which they have confidence. Constituencies who believe powerfully in the mission of the nonprofit organization will give more money than they would if they had lesser passions for the organization. More money enables the nonprofit to do more mission-based work in the community. Simply put, organizations that seem directionless, lack focus, or do not garner respect from individuals and community members will have real difficulty raising charitable funds regardless of how meaningful their mission-oriented work is.

Organizations that Are Good Stewards

People want to give to nonprofits that make the most of their resources. You may have heard stories about fundraising programs where very little of the money raised actually went to the cause used to raise the funds. How would you feel as a donor if you found out that only $.05 of that dollar you gave went to the cause? How would you feel if you were a donor and found out that $.95 of your dollar went not to the child whose program you were supporting but instead to administrative and overhead costs? Although rational people understand that there will be some costs associated with administrative and overhead expenses, donors do not want to see these costs balloon inordinately and take away the bulk of their contributed support. Nonprofits must constantly balance costs versus impact. Doing it well means having donors excited about contributing to your cause. Doing it poorly means risking losing valuable contributed resources in terms of both volunteer time and money.

Organizations that They Know and Care About

People will give to your organization only if they come to learn and know about it. People cannot give to your nonprofit if they do not know it exists or if they do not have any attachment to it. It is therefore critical that you share the mission of your nonprofit organization through your activities and through your fundraising efforts. During my career, I have worked with several nonprofits that the average community member likely did not even know existed. Imagine that you are a person in the community with philanthropic dollars to contribute. Would you give to a nonprofit organization that you had never heard of and did not know or understand its mission? Of course not. This is why it is imperative that you share your mission and tell your community that you exist and are doing great work that is making the world a better place. Without this step, you are destined to be lesser known and less likely to obtain much needed funding for the work that you are doing. Wouldn't it be shameful if your agency, organization, and clients were without the very services you provide—services that they likely rely on—because you did not get the message out to the community about your organization's mission and needs?

This is a good place in the text to say that if your nonprofit organization is not meeting critical needs in the community and being a good steward of the funds that you raise, then do the whole nonprofit community a favor and do not attempt to raise more money. If your donor base is willing to give you funds after hearing your honest case for giving, then likely you are meeting critical needs and being a good steward. If donors are not willing to give you their funds, then you still have real work to do to win their trust, confidence and money.

Everyone Has a Role in Annual Campaigns

Everyone on your staff and volunteer teams can and should play some active role in the fundraising process. By understanding and implementing systems and processes that support both staff and volunteers in their fundraising efforts, you can maximize the amount of funding that your nonprofit organization can obtain from your community. Without implementing systems of support and focus for each group, your staff and volunteers will likely be confused regarding their roles and diminished performance will result. Depending on your organizational structure, fundraising in your nonprofit may be more staff driven or more volunteer driven. Having well-defined fundraising roles, for both staff and volunteers, leads to better communication, understanding, and work product. Having poorly defined roles leads to miscommunication, frustration, and reduced fundraising performance.

Staff Members

For any fundraising process to be as successful as possible, there should be synergy between staff and volunteers. Ideally, staff handles certain roles while volunteers focus on others. When each group knows its role, each can focus their work to generate and attain greater results.

Generally, as a rule of thumb, staff focus on the systems and processes necessary to make fundraising happen. While there are exceptions to every rule, especially in very small nonprofit organizations, most nonprofits utilize staff to design, coordinate, schedule, and guide the process of fundraising at their nonprofit. This ensures that someone's primary purpose is to make sure that fundraising happens, and that it happens effectively. At a major university, there might be dozens or even hundreds of people who do this important work. At a very small nonprofit with no paid staff, this individual might be a volunteer. For most nonprofits, it makes sense to have or hire a professional staff member who has these duties as one of their primary responsibilities. In the case of most nonprofits with very small budgets, this individual is the executive director or chief executive officer (CEO). Once the organizational budget expands, a development person is often hired to help broaden the scope and impact of the organization's fundraising efforts.

Nonprofit staff typically have campaign responsibilities such as:

- Organizing office systems and processes
- Organizing and keeping timelines
- Helping identify volunteers
- Helping to train and motivate volunteers
- Helping volunteers be successful at fundraising
- Preparing case statement materials and other campaign information
- Preparing pledge cards for use in the campaign
- Organizing mail, telephone and other electronic communications and solicitations

As you can see, fundraising tasks that involve organization and logistics are most likely to be planned, organized and completed by staff. Keeping critical organizational work in the hands of staff helps to ensure that the campaign is kept on task and moving forward.

Keys to Staff Success in the Annual Support Campaign

Staff should:

- *Encourage and develop networking opportunities for volunteers alone as well as jointly between staff and volunteers.* Networking and building relationships is important to many volunteers, and this needs to be built in to agendas and planning.

- *Create and implement best practice–based processes for raising funds* (such as the annual support campaign).

- *Require volunteers to be responsible for the results of their efforts.* Just like employees, volunteers should be held accountable to attain whatever results they agreed to when taking their volunteer position at the start of the campaign effort.

- *Help to ensure that fundraising efforts are as fun and uplifting as possible.* People volunteer to feel valued and give back to the world in which they live. Staff should help make volunteers treasure and enjoy this experience, and want to do it again and again.

- *Provide the materials necessary to carry out the tasks related to fundraising.* Whether brochures, pledge cards, or other resources, staff should make sure that volunteers have what they need to be successful.

- *Make volunteers feel and know when they are successful.* Let your volunteers know when they are doing great work and also help them suc-ceed when they may be falling short of expectations. Hardworking vol-unteers always welcome congratulations and open communications.

- *Make sure that staff and volunteers are recognized for their efforts.* Whether a "great job" phone call from the CEO or an "attaboy" in the hallway, make and take opportunities to appreciate strong efforts.

- *Make sure that campaign details are clear and are followed through.* Issues like billing, record keeping, prospect record updating, and other key detail-oriented tasks are traditionally staff roles. Regard-less of who actually does these tasks at your nonprofit, staff are ulti-mately responsible for making sure these activities are handled with professionalism and appropriate confidentiality, detail, etc.

- *Be ultimately responsible for making sure that campaign efforts stay on task.*

(continued)

- *Coach each other on how to improve and help to hold volunteers accountable for their roles before, during, and after the campaign.*
- *Be responsible for keeping campaign efforts on schedule to ensure that volunteers and staff are completing their work in the allotted time.*
- *Set the vision and goals for any campaign effort—but they should do this important task with input from volunteers.* It is unfair to ask volunteers to raise money for a goal that is set solely by staff. Create ownership in this process by involving and engaging volunteers in these integral conversations—whether they are about the critical volunteer recruitment goals or the also important monetary needs of your annual support campaign.

An old management adage states, "If you want to see how employees are treated, watch how they themselves treat the public." You will be far more successful with your entire operation and specifically in the annual campaign, if your employees embody great attitudes and genuine regard for the organization and the mission. Volumes have been written on the benefits of satisfied employees; suffice it to say here that these benefits become tangible when donors graciously give their gifts to your organization in part because of the warm reception they received there.

Managers and organizational leaders have critical roles in annual support, not only because their leadership is needed to organize and oversee the campaign from the staff side, but also because of their key role in staff management and retention overall. If, as a general rule, staff members are not retained long term with the nonprofit, relationships with key donors, prospects, and constituencies will almost always suffer. Imagine a workplace where the average staff member has been there for less than one year. How deep would staff relationships with donors likely be? Having high-quality retained staff members leads to better relationships with your constituency and your entire donor base.

Staff Need to Be Friendly

A management mantra is "Hire attitude, teach skill." Having a staff that is open, receptive, and willing to communicate with people is important for your overall financial development program, not just for the annual support campaign. People who come into contact with your organization need to feel engaged and welcomed into your nonprofit family. Friendly staff can make a tremendous difference in developing and cultivating donor prospect relationships and also in the important work of stewardship with current donors. I do not believe that you can fake being friendly and I have never been a fan of the "smile training" that many nonprofits struggle to teach staff members. If you have people on your staff who are not pleasant with the public, make sure that their jobs are behind the scenes. Each of us has gifts that we bring into the workplace; make sure that your individual employee's talents are truly matched with the position that they hold in your organization. A misplaced staff member can do remarkable damage to a department, donor, prospect or member. A well-placed staff member can open doors that you might never believe could be opened. Staff accordingly and you will help your overall development efforts.

TIPS AND TECHNIQUES

Keys to Hiring Great Staff

My favorite interview questions to find great staff:

- Tell me about yourself.

    Listen closely to what they say and how they say it. Look for why each person fits the culture that you are trying to create in your fundraising program.

- Why should I hire you for this position?

    Again, listen to the answer. See if they speak to issues that are important to you particularly as they relate to passion and excitement for the position and the work. Focusing on their strengths as it relates to the work is also a real positive.

- What are your long-range objectives?

    Listen to see if the position that you are offering is a realistic one for the person's long-term goals and objectives. One of my favorite

(continued)

responses to this question was a financial development candidate that told me that his real passion was to go into modeling. He did not get the position.

- How has your education and experience helped get you ready for this position?

  Listen to how they integrate their life and educational experiences. Especially listen for extracurricular activities that show their passions outside of work. If those interests align, you will likely have a stronger fit for the work.

- Are you a team player?

  While seemingly everyone says yes to this question, ask for examples of how and when they have actually been a team player. Make candidates flesh out real-world examples of why they are the best choice for your team.

- Talk about a time when things did not go the way you wished on a project that you worked on.

  Make the candidate give you an example where something did not go well. Wait as long as you have to in order to get a legitimate answer to this question. Listen to see if the person blames others or takes personal responsibility as appropriate. Did the person learn something from this experience, or does he or she just dismiss it? Mistakes or failures can be tremendous learning tools.

- What is your greatest weakness?

  Listen for how the person answers this question. Is it a vice or personal irresponsibility? Does it show a lack of discipline or focus? Most people will say something like "I work too much" as their pat answer. Do not accept this type of answer without a challenge. Get the applicant to give details about a specific weakness.

- If I were to ask your former coworkers to describe you, what would they say?

  Look for any anxiety on the part of the interviewee and find reasons for any nervousness. This is a great way to see if candidates are uncomfortable with previous work experiences or environments.

- What qualities do you look for in a supervisor?

  If the candidate does not describe qualities you have, then ask yourself if they would be a good fit for your department or your

(continued)

(continued)
organization. Most people will say something like leadership or vision; again, get them to talk about specifics. What qualities about their last supervisor did they like best? What did they like least?

- If you could change one thing about your life, what would you change? This gives you a window into candidates' souls. Look for things that really speak to them. You may see signs of things that went wrong personally or professionally that will also help you to make the best decision for your department and your organization.

Volunteers

Volunteers play critical roles in the annual support campaign fundraising process. Because the roles of volunteers are discussed in depth later in this text, we will not go into full detail here. It is helpful, however, to mention a few key roles for volunteers at this time.

Volunteers should:

- Be advocates for the organization.
- Be able to explain why the nonprofit is vital in the community and why it is deserving of charitable funding. (This is often called "telling the story" of the nonprofit organization as it relates to fundraising.)
- Help raise and steward charitable funds.
- Make a gift to the nonprofit.
- Be willing to solicit others as their relationship to the nonprofit develops and matures.
- Be engaged in helping set goals and objectives for fundraising efforts.
- Help recruit others in the fundraising process.
- Participate in meetings, events, and/or training to understand and be able to fully implement their roles.

It is important to understand at this point that without fundraising volunteers, your nonprofit organization will never glean the most from the efforts made. It does not matter if you have the largest development or advancement department in the world. If you do not engage and involve volunteers in the fundraising process, your organization will never, ever reach its full potential.

Roles the Annual Campaign Plays in Your Nonprofit

There are many reasons to have an annual support campaign, and many of them do not involve money at all. I have often said that a well-run annual support campaign would be worth doing even if it did not raise any contributed funds. The by-products of this effort are so positive that the exercise is worthy of doing even in the absence of raising money. That said, I want you to raise the money too!

Here are some of the many roles that the annual support campaign plays in your nonprofit organization:

- Getting people involved in the work that you do
- Sharing your story with the community
- Encouraging investing (not always in a financial sense) in the critical work that you do
- Encouraging a philanthropic mind-set
- Teaching philanthropy
- Building ownership in your nonprofit
- Discovering staff and volunteer leadership
- Identifying staff and volunteer talent
- Developing and training staff and volunteer leaders
- Building relationships between staff and volunteers
- Explaining the vital work that you do
- Developing, evaluating, and honing the key messages about your organization and what it really does in the community that you are serving
- Sharing the important work that you do with a broader community and getting them to invest in it

Funding Your Mission: Raising Money!

One of the most obvious benefits of the annual support campaign is its ability to raise funds year in and year out. A high-functioning annual support campaign is like having a deep mutual fund of donors. Because your donor base is broad in such a campaign, it is a very stable source of operational and organizational support. A typical annual campaign has a good staff component, a strong board solicitation effort, and a solid major gifts and community gifts division. The range of these funding sources, as well as the diversity of the donors themselves, makes the well-run annual support campaign one of the most reliable funding streams that a nonprofit organization can have in its portfolio. One fact about charitable support that is often overlooked by nonprofit staff and volunteers alike, is the reality that charitable funds are almost always the highest margin program that you have at your organization. A dollar raised in philanthropy almost always does more to help the bottom line than any other increased revenue that you may generate in any other area of your organization.

Involving People in the Work You Do

Few resources are more valuable to a nonprofit organization than that of dedicated staff and volunteers. The annual support campaign helps you to build and develop both groups. Through the campaign experience, staff members learn to personalize and synthesize the mission of your organization. Staff are then able to share this passion with volunteers, who can then communicate these key messages to others in the community. By building a public relations, marketing, and development team, your annual campaign organization assists your overall nonprofit messaging and branding efforts. Involving people in the work that you do makes your nonprofit exponentially more visible and broad reaching.

Encouraging Philanthropy

People need to learn about your organization in order to know that they want to support it and its important work in the community. Most households have a philanthropy budget of some type; rarely do people have an endless supply of funds to simply give away. By sharing the story of your nonprofit mission and work through your annual support campaign, you educate individuals and families about your valuable services and encourage them to support these efforts financially. This is an important act for both the giver and the receiver. Without philanthropic assistance, most nonprofits are virtually impossible to operate. If we do not inform the public about our mission, they may never know about a program they would love to support. We cheat ourselves, our community and the donors themselves if we do not help prospective donors to know about the work that we do and the value it serves to the broader good.

Teaching Philanthropy

Philanthropy is practiced in many faiths, countries, and cultures. While it is a value that is taught in various ways, actually helping others to see the benefits of philanthropy in your own nonprofit can be a critical part of your organization's short and long term success. By teaching staff and volunteers the need for charitable gifts to your nonprofit, you are helping to perpetuate your mission. Also, by educating staff and volunteers how to be successful at fundraising, you are, in essence, preparing them to have a more successful and self reliant future by helping to ensure that the organization can sustain itself. Self reliant nonprofit organizations that have good fundraising skills in their staff and volunteers, are more likely to survive in good times and bad and are more likely to be able to sustain downward turns in the economy or other challenges moving forward. The results of teaching philanthropy can be very exciting and are likely to have long-lasting benefits for your own organization as well as others in the nonprofit sector.

Building Ownership

As people learn about who you are and what you do, some will choose to become more deeply involved in your work as co-owners and co-investors. These individuals value the work that you do enough to invest their limited resources into making your critical mission-based work happen in the community. Whether your mission is as a university teaching the public or as an environmental organization preserving the earth, identifying and engaging owner investors in your nonprofit work can and will reap great dividends. I have found that when people use personal pronoun references, such as "my" or "our" when speaking about your organization, you are well on your way to building co-owners and co-investors. There is little that is more valuable, in terms of donor cultivation or stewardship, than a person who says to a friend, "I want you to come see my nonprofit organization where I volunteer. Our community is so fortunate to have this organization."

Discovering Leadership

One of the best ways to identify current and future nonprofit leaders is through the annual support campaign. Think of the type of person you wish you could get on your board of directors. Wouldn't you love your next board member to be a great fundraiser? Then why not field test prospective board members as volunteers in your annual support campaign? A good board member has many responsibilities outside of fundraising, but having board members who are willing to be active and involved in the commendable work of philanthropy is extremely important to nonprofit organizations. Engaging people outside of your board alone will make for a more effective and higher-functioning annual support campaign. The diversity achieved by developing and including people outside your board is an invaluable asset. Your organization may have the chance to tap into people or organizations that, before this, had not even known about your highly admirable work. When utilizing volunteers outside of your board, a high-functioning annual support campaign helps your nonprofit to identify future and current leaders for your fundraising, your committees and your board. This strategy also identifies people who are good storytellers about your mission and passionate about your cause in general. These individuals can be great assets in many ways other than just in the arena of fundraising.

Volunteers who are good storytellers can help in other areas of public relations. For example, they can:

- Work with and represent your group to politicians.

- Interact with foundations.

- Talk to civic clubs such as Rotary, Lions, and so on.

- Be involved in donor and prospect visits.

- Help out with special events or other efforts.

- Serve on committees at your nonprofit.

- Countless other possibilities!

Proper utilization of volunteer resources can bring multiple benefits to your nonprofit organization. While your volunteer leaders are helping your organization, they are also becoming more engaged in your programs and mission. This often has compounding benefits. As people become more involved, they have a deeper understanding of the work that you do, the need for that work and ultimately become even more committed to seeing the organization succeed. While the volunteers gain this valuable knowledge and experience, they are also simultaneously helping you! It is truly a win-win situation for your mission and your efforts.

Identifying Talent

Undiscovered talents most likely exist within the staff and volunteers of your nonprofit. While you may have recruited or hired a particular staff member or volunteer because of a certain characteristic or skill, this does not mean that this is their only talent. The annual support campaign can help you to see and identify these possibly hidden talents in your staff and volunteers. Some people are great askers while others are great facilitators and team leaders. Still others prefer to be part of the organizational efforts of the group and the campaign as a whole. Everyone has a skill or talent to bring to the annual support campaign. Your job is to find out what that talent is and put it to great use!

It is truly a rare individual who is great at everything or has all of the qualities that we are seeking for a volunteer or staff position. Virtually everyone has strengths and weaknesses for both better and worse. The next list outlines some characteristics of great fundraising staff and volunteers, but, remember, the list is neither exclusive nor exhaustive. You want the best people that you can find for each position in your fundraising effort. The list can help you identify who those people might be.

Some of the skills that make for strong fundraisers include:

- Ability to listen well
- Willingness to accept coaching and learn
- Enjoys conversing with people
- Positive attitude
- Knowing when to ask for help
- Capable of dealing with and managing stress
- Ability to motivate others
- Willingness to work toward a goal
- Comfortable talking with strangers or meeting new people
- Good organizational skills
- Works well with other team members
- Strong verbal and written communicator

This list does not describe every outstanding fundraiser I have ever met. It does, however, give some strong indicators for individuals who may be more natural at cultivating prospects and performing other campaign tasks. These traits can be helpful in identifying volunteers and staff people who might make good fundraisers.

Now that you have seen some of the qualities that strong fundraisers might possess, take a look at some of the volunteers already involved with your organization. You likely have some great people already in the midst of your nonprofit work who are volunteering for you in other areas of your organization. Maybe you just have not looked at them before as potential fundraisers. The next exercise can help you identify possible volunteers both inside and outside of your nonprofit.

Exercise

Determining Your Volunteer Wish List

Who are your best volunteers in any area today?

List your top 10 volunteers at your organization.

1.
2.
3.
4.
5.
6.
7.
8.
9.
10.

Many of the individuals above might make great fundraising volunteers in your annual support campaign. They likely share passion and commitment to the work that you do and are already giving you their most precious asset—time. People who are willing to invest their time with you are also very likely to be willing to invest their money. They also are possibly willing to help you with other projects that are important to your organization, in addition to the work that they are already doing. The annual support campaign just may be a great place for them to contribute additional time, talent and treasure.

Now think hard about the people who are not yet involved with your organization. Do not be concerned at this point about how to get these people involved; just identify them in the next list. Just think about the

---

(continued)

individuals in your community whom you wish would be involved two years from now. (Tip: Think strategically about who in your community could help you most.)

1.
2.
3.
4.
5.
6.
7.
8.
9.
10.

Work beyond this effort with your senior management and other staff and volunteer teams to list people *within* your organizational sphere of influence who might likely make great fundraisers. Make time to plan how to engage and involve these people in the worthy work of fundraising and the annual support campaign. There will be more on how to do this in Chapters 5, 6, and 7.

Also, work with your staff and volunteers to list people in your broader community who would likely make good fundraisers if you could get them involved with your organization. How can you work toward having a better and stronger list of volunteers now and in the future?

Developing and Training Leaders

Who are the best trainers on staff in your organization? Who are the best volunteer trainers in your organization? You can utilize both groups in your annual support campaign. Before and during every annual support campaign, staff and volunteers must be trained on what to do and how to do it during the campaign. Giving seasoned staff members and volunteer leaders the opportunity to work in front of groups to teach them the processes and procedures allows more experienced staff and volunteers the opportunity to build and develop presentation and leadership skills. Because the annual support campaign happens every year, there are annual opportunities for people to learn to become great trainers or hone their existing training skills. Additionally, having staff members and volunteers do the instructing, allows them to share their stories, their knowledge and be recognized for their expertise. Having and growing annual support campaign trainers within your nonprofit, is essentially building your leaders of today and for tomorrow.

There are many training opportunities in an annual support campaign. The next list gives just a few ways that training can be utilized.

- Face-to-face training
- One-on-One Training
- Group training
- Online training
- Webinars offering workshops or classes on how to fundraise
- Campaign updates and tips throughout the campaign effort
- Staff training of volunteers
- Seasoned volunteers training volunteers or staff as appropriate
- Other?!

As you can see, there are many opportunities for individuals to try out, improve, and expand their capacity to train others. The annual support campaign is a great place for both staff and volunteers to share their gifts related to training others in annual support and fundraising.

Here are just a few topics that individuals can be trained on. These concepts are explained and expanded later in the text.

- How to make "an ask"
- What your nonprofit needs money for
- How your organization spent the charitable dollars it received last year
- Key people in the organization to turn to if they have a question

- Where money that your nonprofit receives goes, and who is helped
- Programs that would not exist if you did not raise these charitable dollars
- Programs that would have to be cut if you did not raise these funds
- How much money you are trying to raise and for what purpose
- How to fill out a pledge card to make a gift
- The types of payments your organization accepts
- The companies that match gifts to your organization

The list of possibilities is as long as the questions that a new staff member or volunteer might ask. It is important to remember also that learning does not occur just because you have had or offered a training class. People learn differently, and at different paces. Having multiple training programs, as well as multiple trainers, increases the likelihood that your participants will learn and then be able to implement your key messages. Offering people opportunities to learn, follow up, and ask questions whenever possible is integral to the success of your campaign. Make certain that volunteers and staff who have just been trained know whom to contact and are made to feel welcomed when they have further questions. Often until we are actually doing a task, we are not aware of the questions we might have. This follow-up is also a perfect time for the lead staff or senior volunteer to provide positive reinforcement and motivation for the new participant.

Building Relationships with Donors and Volunteers

The annual support campaign provides a great way to build relationships among staff and volunteers. As these two groups unite around a common cause, they have a tremendous opportunity to get to know each other and to work together. The bonds that are formed through training events, campaign celebrations, and common goals are priceless relationships that often would not be created otherwise. I have relationships with individuals whom I worked with on my first annual support campaigns. They are friends and colleagues whose friendships I hold in great value to this day. Indeed, some of the people I respect most in this world are individuals with whom I have worked on fundraising campaigns. Typically, individuals who work on annual support campaigns care deeply about helping others. These same people make wonderful friends and colleagues in life, and these are the people who you want to have involved in your organization.

Some ways to build relationships with donors and prospects:

- Take or meet people for coffee or tea to talk about your organization.
- Take or meet people for lunch.
- If you have an organization that involves people, talk to them during engagement with your organization.
- Talk with people at or around an event.
- Build relationships with people during volunteer activities.
- Encourage networking among volunteers and staff at functions that you hold for your organization.
- Use the telephone to call people and build relationships.
- Utilize tools like email and instant messaging as appropriate to build relationships
- Handwritten notes mean so much in today's society. Write more notes to key people in your organization.
- Consider connecting with people around key events in their lives, such as birthdays, anniversaries, graduations, and the like.

We discuss methods for donor and prospect cultivation and relationship building later in this text. For now understand that by implementing and developing your annual support campaign, you are also taking a vital opportunity to build relationships with your donors and volunteers. People who are volunteering to help build your nonprofit organization through their work on your annual support campaign will also become many of your best donors. Their commitment of time will convey into their giving of gifts—often very large gifts—to your organization as well. As you grow your volunteer base, you will simultaneously be growing your donor base.

Explaining What Your Organization Really Does

An added result of the annual support campaign is that it allows your organization to fully explain to the public what it really does in the community it serves. Often, especially in today's nonprofit world, only part of the nonprofit business generates revenue. Whether you run programs for people who are visually impaired or provide meals to those unable to get around, many in the general public may believe that your nonprofit organization somehow pays for itself through the fees it charges for services. While this is sometimes the case, there is almost always another side to the issue that the public does not regularly consider. Hospitals provide care to the indigent. Transitional housing programs provide homes for those who need it for any number of different reasons. Scores of agencies provide assistance to those with medical or physical challenges. The list is almost endless; the public needs to be reminded of the critical work that you do that is not fully funded through other means. Your charitable mission needs to be in the forefront of people's minds. The annual support campaign is yet another way to get that mission in front of your constituency and public. That is what we call "telling the story" or explaining the "case for support" for the organization.

 TIPS AND TECHNIQUES

There are lots of creative ways to get your message out. Consider these:

- Share testimonials of people who have seen or felt the direct impact of what you do. There is nothing quite as powerful as people's stories of benefit from your organization. They can make impressions that spur others to action.

- Explain how much you need people to be involved in your work. Demonstrate that their help and assistance has real value to the community and to your organization.

- Talk about something that is inherently memorable about your organization or efforts. Special stories, people, events, and circumstances can all be potent parts of effective messaging efforts.

(continued)

- Show how your efforts are being replicated by others if appropriate.
- Present true stories of life changing work to make points to individuals and groups that do not fully understand the work that you do.
- Use a symbol to create an image of what you are trying to do. (Do not do this too often, though, or audiences get confused and the images will lose their value).
- Compare how the world is changed through the work you do with be-fore-and-after contrasts.
- Demonstrate how what you do makes the world a better place.
- Illustrate something that makes your organization or effort unique and separates your organization from others doing similar work.
- Display how your work has brought about a positive outcome in the past.

Developing Communications

A major benefit of the annual campaign is that it gives you the opportunity every year to restate and hone your communications to the public. This is your chance to shape, tell, and evaluate the great work that you are doing in the community. By revisiting the work that you are doing and the messaging surrounding your work, you make sure that your board, staff, and volunteer base are all in sync about what it is you do and why it is imperative. Working on "telling your story" every year leads to a more focused mission, a clearer message, and a stronger comprehension, by the public, of what it is you really do. When people truly assimilate information, they are able to explain it in their own words and with their own internal passion. One benefit of the repetition of the annual campaign is that staff, board members, and volunteers get to share and repeat their story. This exercise allows the tellers to perfect their stories to be most effectual over time. These volunteers and donors also hear others explain the mission in a different way which allows them to improve their own understanding and comprehension. Hearing others speaking so emphatically about the work that you do often makes donors and volunteers become more deeply engaged. This process can lead to even deeper immersion in your organization and larger gifts from your volunteers and donors.

For each audience that you are trying to reach, you should have a specific communications strategy. It just makes sense to communicate in ways that each audience is most ready to embrace. This is not to say that you need a different strategy to communicate with each group. Merging communications strategies may make a great deal of sense when groups require or benefit from similar communications.

Some groups that you might want to customize your message for or include in your communications strategies include:

- Board
- Committees
- General donors
- Major donors
- Prospects
- Staff
- Fundraising volunteers
- Newspapers
- Television stations
- Radio stations
- Internet users/Web site communications
- Email recipients
- Newsletter recipients
- Billboard, flyers, poster, and signage readers
- Participants in other programs or areas of your organization
- Corporations
- Foundations
- Other?

As you can see, you might develop several different communications strategies in order to meet the needs of several different audiences. Each of the audiences might also be viewed from the perspective of:

- Age

- Gender

- Race

- Occupation

- Interest (such as whales, seals, climate change, etc., in an environmental organization)

- Program area interest (children's programs, elderly, animals, parishioners, etc.)

- Other?

Again, you can divide up communication audiences into various groups and segments; the most effective organizations take varying interests, issues, and groups into account when they create their communications plans. If you are a larger nonprofit with significant resources, consider creating communications plans for as many of the listed audiences and groups that you can. If you are a smaller nonprofit with very limited resources, consider creating materials and messages that embrace your key audiences as comprehensively as possible. Staff, volunteers, and consultants from the marketing arena can help you to make sure that you are doing the best you can with the resources available. Do not be afraid to ask for help from volunteers or area firms that may specialize or have expertise in marketing and communications. In today's high-communication world, there may be experts within your midst who would be willing to help you for little or no cost.

In each communication, consider things like:

- Language (Is it engaging and readable?)

- Pictures or photographs

- Wording (Avoid acronyms that are unfamiliar to people who do not know your organization well.)

- Production costs

- General impression (Does it look too pricey? Does it make the overall impression that you would like?)

- Mail concerns, such as:

  - Postage costs

  - Envelope concerns (such as size or cost)

  - Will it be opened or read?

Certainly there are other things to consider when putting together your communications strategies, but the information in this section has hopefully given you a much greater understanding of the possible impact of a well-run annual support campaign communications program.

Roles of the Annual Campaign in Your Overall Financial Development Program

Donor Entry Point

A major role of the annual support campaign is to introduce and obtain first-time donors to your organization. The campaign lets people in your constituency and in your community know that the organization is seeking contributed support and that it needs their assistance to fulfill integral program needs. It also tells donors and prospects why their gifts are important and needed by the organization. Annual support campaigns let donors and prospects know how their gifts will benefit the nonprofit, the community, and the constituency served.

Regularly asking donors and prospects to make gifts through the annual support campaign also enables the organization to routinely and regularly thank prospects-turned-donors for their gifts. Often, donors' first gifts to your organization are through the annual campaign. The campaign allows your organization to educate your donors and your donors to educate you—if you are willing to take the time to listen.

Developing Your Overall Donor Base

Another positive role of the annual support campaign is that it helps you to *develop* your overall donor base. By *develop,* I mean that it helps you grow donors from small, less committed donors to larger, more committed ones. The campaign does this in several ways. It creates a simple and easy method for people to give repeatedly to your nonprofit. When an individual gives a one-time gift to an organization, it can be a chance occurrence; it may not represent significant attachment by the donor to the organization. A repeat gift is less likely to be a fluke or an anomaly on the part of the donor. This repeat giving gives the nonprofit organization additional opportunities to thank and report back to the donor on how the gift was used, and also to begin to understand the donor's motivations for making the repeat gifts. By sharing what the donor's gift has made possible, the nonprofit can deepen its relationship with the donor. Continued contact also enables the nonprofit to encourage and engage the donor in other aspects of the organization's work. Donors can be asked to assist with different programs or be shown further projects that might be of interest to them. This highly effective method of engagement often leads to higher gifts to the annual support campaign or to other parts of the financial development program. Remember, the more you connect donors to your organization by igniting their passion, their level of allegiance, loyalty, responsibility and duty will all increase. This can translate into great things for your organization.

Donor Recognition

The annual support campaign enables your organization to identify and understand how donors think and act through their philanthropy. Because the annual campaign occurs every year, there is tremendous opportunity to use the campaign to learn, know, and understand what your donors feel and what is important to them as people and as contributors. One key avenue for this growth in understanding is donor recognition. How do your donors want to be recognized, if at all? Donor recognition can be highly personalized and does not have to be limited to the traditional names on the plaque in the office lobby. While some donors strive and are highly concerned with donor recognition, others care significantly less about having their names up in lights. Virtually all donors, however, expect to receive some sort of personal thanks for their gift to a nonprofit. Personalize how you recognize and show thanks to your donors.

Creating and implementing good acknowledgement and stewardship practices in your annual support campaign helps to lay the groundwork for stronger donor relationships in all aspects of your financial development program. Getting acknowledgement, stewardship and donor recognition right in the annual support campaign not only helps make your donors happy in the short term, but it also helps you set the stage for other development efforts such as capital, major gifts and endowment work.

 TIPS AND TECHNIQUES

Some great ways to recognize donors and volunteers:

- Personally thank them with a handwritten letter, a phone call, a personal visit, all of the above or something else. But personally thank them.
- Hand-deliver a personal recognition to them at their home or office.
- List them on a plaque or wall in a prominent place if the donor okays it.
- Consider dedicating a meeting space, conference room or other space to a special donor who has had lasting impact on your organization.
- Dedicate outdoor spaces, such as trees, gardens, or walkways, to major donors.
- Write about donors and volunteers in your newsletters and through your print media.
- Identify special donors or volunteers with special designations at events, meetings, or other gatherings. For example, use name tags of different colors or special table seating to honor these individuals and families.

(continued)

- Encourage them to be involved in other areas of your nonprofit organization. Consider getting donors and volunteers to participate in areas of your nonprofit that they might not otherwise be involved. Consider inviting and honoring volunteers or donors at an event that they might not ordinarily have attended. This enables both the honoree and the event attendees to see or be reminded of the diverse areas of your organization and the many facets of the work that is done throughout the year.
- Invite these individuals to serve on committee, task forces, or even the board as appropriate.
- Other ideas? Remember to make recognition personal and meaningful to the donors. If you make it thoughtful and appropos for them, you will do it well.

Culture of Philanthropy

The annual support campaign helps your organization to create a culture of philanthropy that carries over into other areas of development, such as capital and planned giving. It is hard to ask someone for a large gift (whatever that means to them . . . whether $100 or $100 million) if you have never asked them for a smaller one. This is not to say that it cannot be done, but for most people, relationships occur and deepen over time. If you think of donor engagement as courtship before marriage, annual support campaigns provide the time to court the donors and prospects and get to know them rather than just walking up to them and asking for their hand in marriage. The annual campaign enables you to get to know your donors and for them to get to know you. This valuable relationship–building process provides you with critical information that may be of even greater value to the organization when seeking very large annual, capital, or planned gifts. I often say to organizations with which I am working: "Would you rather make a mistake on a $100 ask or a $100,000 ask?" (I prefer to make my mistakes smaller!) Annual campaigns provide the opportunity to get nos from donors when the stakes are smaller and the relationship is still developing. A "no" from a donor allows us to learn and identify how we can improve or adjust our service (if appropriate) to better connect with or serve our donors and our population. We want to get these nos when the stakes are smallest so that we are able to discover and work on these donors and prospects again until we get yeses.

Large gifts are rarely received overnight. Even though we all hear of stories where a nonprofit organization is left funds in a will or is given an extremely large gift "out of thin air," these stories are true exceptions. Truly transformational gifts—those that make organizational change really happen—are usually the result of years of involvement and engagement between an organization and a donor. We discuss this more in Chapter 7; but here it is important to understand that the annual support campaign plays a valuable role in donor and prospect development and cultivation.

Helps Identify Prospects for Larger Gifts

Your largest donors to annual support campaigns often become your largest donors to capital campaigns and other major giving initiatives. Many, if properly cultivated and solicited, will eventually become planned giving and endowment donors as well. By learning and recognizing who in your constituency likes you enough to support you regularly and meaningfully, you are setting the stage for larger and more significant gifts over time. These gifts may be more substantial annual support gifts, capital gifts for large physical plant improvements, or other major gifts of meaning to the donor or the nonprofit organization. One sure sign of a good nonprofit/donor relationship is repeated gifts over time. The annual campaign lets you identify individuals over a period of years who like and regard your organization enough to support it financially. These same donors usually make the best prospects for other major projects (such as capital projects or endowment building).

IN THE REAL WORLD

A donor named John gave his first gift to an annual support campaign. John's $25 donation was a heartfelt gift to the nonprofit that helped children and families. Over the last 15 years or so, John has made increasingly significant gifts to this organization, leading to a $10,000 gift to this year's annual support campaign. It is fun to look at his donor record and see that literally, every year, his gift grew more. His $25 initial gift has grown to help many children and families now.

What is not surprising is how John's increasing gift correlates almost exactly with his involvement with the organization. As John has grown older, so have his resources. He is now a successful businessman; he was a young man just out of college when he made his first gift. Over the years, his love for and appreciation of the nonprofit organization have grown. As he has been involved with and heard the story of the nonprofit, he has become increasingly motivated to give more and more.

The annual support campaign has given John an annual education, first as a donor and then as a volunteer, about the vital work that this organization accomplishes in its community. John has since given large capital campaign gifts and has written the nonprofit into his will. Without the annual support campaign to involve and educate John about the charitable mission, none of this might have occurred.

Shows the Value of Your Mission Year In and Year Out

By sharing the mission of your organization every year in a highly intentional way, you remind your donors, constituency, and general public of the inherent value of the essential work that you do. People are especially busy in today's society. The ability to remind people of your organization and deepen their understanding of it over time remains key. Through the annual support campaign, not only are people reminded that your work remains necessary, but also they are given the opportunity to support it financially. You must remind your community of the work that you do so that they can dedicate and extend themselves and their families in support of your efforts. If you do not remind your donors of the noteworthy work that your organization is doing, others will remind them about the work of their organizations, and they will get the donors' charitable dollars.

Staff Learn the Value of Philanthropy

A further worthy role of the annual support campaign is the teaching of staff the necessity of philanthropy to the organization. Without teaching and practice, staff members do not learn how to raise contributed funds, nor do they practice the skills and theories of philanthropy in general. Teaching and practicing philanthropy forms a solid foundation for our organizations, as we grow and develop the next phase of nonprofit leaders. By sharing with staff and volunteers how to implement and successfully run annual support campaigns, we are ensuring that our nonprofits will flourish well into the foreseeable future. Staff members need to discover, and be taught, how to raise and steward charitable contributions. The annual support campaign provides a marvelous training ground for such practice.

Over the years, I have worked with some employees in the nonprofit sector who believe that the title of the job for which they were hired encompasses their total job description. By this I mean that, say, the individuals thinks that because he was hired as a business office manager or as a case manager, that type of work is all he must offer to the nonprofit. In my experience, this is anything but correct.

Properly worded employee job descriptions outline that part of every position is involving and promoting philanthropy at the nonprofit organization. Identifying and connecting with volunteers, in addition to helping with the work of fundraising, is everyone's job in the ideal nonprofit environment.

By hiring to this job description, you achieve clear communications and expectations before, during, and after the hiring process is completed. If you do not communicate this clearly at the time of hire, you risk getting someone who is a good employee in one area but believes that fundraising is everyone else's job. Great nonprofit employees actively participate in philanthropy at their organizations. Make sure to hire people who will help you to get this work done.

Volunteers Learn about the Importance of Philanthropy

Just as staff members need training and learning opportunities, volunteers do as well. The annual support campaign is an excellent venue for all volunteers to get more experience in and more confident at fundraising. This is the time when volunteers learn about the full depth and breadth of the services that you provide. This is the opportunity to teach and share passion about the organization for which they choose to spend their precious time. This is the place for volunteers to gather the skill on how to ask for a gift. This is also the occasion for them to build self-confidence and see firsthand the most effective ways to solicit and raise contributed funds. If you create and promote a culture in which the annual support campaign is a group effort, where training and support are available for both staff and volunteers, your campaign will be substantially more successful and more highly rewarding. Together, staff, volunteers, donors, and even prospects can all learn about the values and annual support needs of the organization.

Staff and Volunteers Benefit from Annual Campaign Experience

Staff and volunteers should expect a lot from their annual support campaign experience. The work is not easy, but there are real returns to staff and volunteers from the annual support campaign experience.

TIPS AND TECHNIQUES

What should staff and volunteers expect from their annual campaign experience?

- Leadership experience
- Opportunity to improve management skills
- Chance to accomplish meaningful service

(continued)

> *(continued)*
> - Arena to learn or sharpen their fundraising skills
> - Increased sense of ownership and commitment in the mission
> - Friends
> - Pride in their effort and their organization
> - Positive impact on the world
> - Knowledge that they are giving back to the community in a meaningful way

Develop Volunteer Leadership Experience

Annual support campaigns provide volunteers and staff alike with the setting to lead and motivate others. Selecting and prompting key individuals in your organization to have leadership opportunities empowers your nonprofit to first discover and then ultimately field test leadership candidates in your organization. Volunteers can be given the chance to lead during the annual support campaign. If they do well, they might be nominated to the board of directors. By giving people the chance to lead during the annual support campaign, you are growing the leadership capabilities of your volunteer and staff teams to the betterment of your current and future organization.

Increase Staff Leadership and Management Skills

Designated staff members who may be management candidates for future job openings can be given the opportunity to train, lead, or work with key volunteers and volunteer teams. Staff members can be given the opportunity to grow through their annual support duties and strong performance may lead to future advancement within the organization or in the nonprofit community at large. As we outline later, there are many places for staff members to develop and practice their leadership and management skills in the annual support campaign.

Accomplish Meaningful Mission Service

Who among us does not like to feel as if we have made the world a better place at the end of the day? Many people want to know that they have made a difference in making the world a brighter and better place for others. Not all people work in a job where they feel this satisfaction every day. For some, work is a tedious way to make enough money to live. Some are so far away from the end result that it is hard to see the direct benefit of their work in society. Their jobs lack the fulfillment inherent in other occupations that help others. By engaging people as volunteers in the annual support campaign, we can give them the chance to experience the joy and gratification of making a difference through their community service. The old adage that you get back tenfold what you give is so true in volunteering. Just think, you are giving that possibility to people in your community!

The reasons that people give time to charitable organizations are the same ones that make them give their hard-earned funds. People give for a variety of reasons; it is our job to help find out what makes the prospect in front of you want to volunteer. Work in intentional volunteer development is likely to pay off for years to come if you are willing to invest in the time and energy to identify and recruit high-quality volunteers. There will be more on this topic discussed in Chapter 5.

Improve Ability to Raise Funds

It is tremendously rewarding to watch people's confidence grow as they gain the experience and gratification of working in the annual support campaign. It is wonderful to see the satisfaction of individuals as they learn that they too can become capable fundraisers and feel the joy of a positive experience and solicitation. The first time a person gets a gift from a donor can be a very gratifying experience. It can also lead to increased confidence in other areas of a person's life. Watching volunteers and staff members become better and more self-assured communicators is just another by product of a well-run and organized annual support campaign.

Increase Pride and Ownership

When volunteers and staff members become co-owners of the organization, great things happen. Staff and volunteers feel a great sense of pride when they know that the work that they have performed is directly helping to increase the mission of the organization and the community that it serves.

There are many reasons why people give to causes:

- *Care and concern for others.* Giving helps to ensure that the lives of others are improved.

- *Habit.* Often, giving comes from one's upbringing or cultural background and individuals continue to give out of habit, custom, duty or beliefs.

- *Tax benefits.* Depending on the country in which you live, there can be tax benefits for giving to charity.

- *Respect for the person asking.* When someone you respect asks you for help with something, it is easy to say yes.

- *Someone asked.* Think about the last charitable contribution that you made. Did someone ask you to give it? Probably so!

- *They are involved.* When people become involved in charitable work, they often get excited to support it through their time, talent, and treasure.

- *They want to preserve their values.* People want things that are important to them to continue and advance as causes. Giving to organizations that support their values helps to make the world better in their eyes.

- *They want to repay a debt.* Many people feel that they have been blessed by someone or something that gave them things they needed in life. The motivation to give back to the society that has given them such a good life is often strong.

- *They have guilt.* Some feel guilty over things that they have done or over things they have done, unfortunate occurrences that have occurred, or over breaks that they have been given in life. Giving helps alleviate this guilt.

- *They want or desire peer recognition.* Some give to be recognized and appreciated by their peers. Often people will consider giving more in order to achieve some recognition or status level in the community. Their name being prominently displayed, on a plaque, at a high giving level, or next to an esteemed colleague may be an influential factor.

- *They want or need to belong and to join others.* Most people like to belong to organizations that make them feel special or valued. Joining others helps people to feel a part of something larger than themselves.

- *They want to improve their community.* Some people give just to make the community they live a better place. This has long been the spirit of corporations as well as individual philanthropists in general

- *In memory.* Often when loved ones pass away, family or friends will give to a charity or organization that has been significant to the deceased in some way.

Summary

The annual support campaign plays many significant and vital roles in the life of your nonprofit organization. Donors give to organizations that they trust, respect, and believe will be good stewards of their contributed dollars. Staff and volunteers alike can grow and benefit from participating in the annual support campaign. Whether making friends, building confidence, or gaining skills that will make their nonprofit experiences more complete, everyone can learn and grow through their involvement in the annual support campaign.

People volunteer in fundraising campaigns for many reasons. For some, it is giving back to the community and world in which they live; for others, it is because of the intangible benefits that they receive. While some are jockeying on a personal, social status competition, others give out of a sense of habit or duty. Whatever the reasons, philanthropy, and its practice, is a vital part of the nonprofit sector and makes the world we live in more fulfilling.

The annual campaign also plays a central role in the philanthropic process as a whole in a nonprofit organization. Annual campaigns remain the entry point for many donors as they learn about and become more involved in the mission at a particular nonprofit. For many, annual campaigns are the first step from which they grow into capital and planned giving donors. First-time annual support campaign contributions often represent the beginning of long and happy relationships between donors and the organizations to which they contribute.

Annual campaigns also serve to bring focus to nonprofit organizations as they unite on the integral marketing and communications plans which help tell the public who they are and what they do. By bringing both attention and definition to the organization's key charitable messaging, the annual support campaign makes sure that this critical marketing and communication effort is reviewed and analyzed on a yearly basis.

Annual support campaigns help to bring together volunteers and staff members around the mission-oriented work of helping others through philanthropy. This process makes the organization, and the community that it serves, stronger by tapping into and involving people in the organizational efforts and work in the community. When people give to a nonprofit organization, they are showing their support and endorsing the central work of that organization. This brings value to both the nonprofit and the individual who is making the gift.

Annual support campaigns are a fundamental component of any nonprofit organization's development program. There should be an opportunity for donors, volunteers, and staff to run, manage, and implement an annual support campaign every year.

## CHAPTER 3

Assessing Campaign Readiness

After reading this chapter, you will be able to:

- Understand the various aspects of being ready to do an annual support campaign.
- Recognize the readiness of your nonprofit organization to do an annual campaign.
- Begin formulating ideas around the tasks and activities related to getting your organization as ready as it can be.

Your organization has looked at the benefits of doing a well-run annual support campaign, and you have decided to move forward. How do you know if you are ready?

There are many components to operating a successful annual support campaign, and it is unlikely that you will ever have all of them in place before beginning. I have worked with literally hundreds of annual support campaigns, and I can tell you from experience that I have never had one that went what I would call perfectly. With that said, you cannot wait until everything in your annual support campaign world is perfect. You must—at some point—take the step to *doing* an annual support campaign.

I tell you this because the best time to raise money of any kind is when you and your organization are ready. Still, you cannot wait until conditions are perfect. If you wait until conditions are absolutely right, you will never go out and tell the story of your organization and make "the ask" of people and organizations for resources to support you. It just will not happen.

I want you to commit to erring on the side of *doing* an annual support campaign. As we have discussed in earlier chapters, this is an opportunity for your organization to build philanthropy as well as to learn the critical skills necessary to be successful in fundraising overall. This is the time to engage volunteers, to try asking for a gift, and to tell the story of the great work that your organization is doing every day in your community. This is the time to move this initiative forward. The best time to have an annual support campaign is every year. Ideally, that trend begins with this year if it is not already a tradition at your non-profit organization.

There are many things that, if you have them, will make your annual support campaign easier. Again, in working with hundreds of campaigns, I have very rarely, if ever, had campaigns that had all of these things. As each component is discussed, I will attempt to stress those that I feel are most important. Building an annual support campaign is like building anything else. You can build it out of different things depending on what you have available. Use your strengths and adapt accordingly, without taking away from the best practice concepts that are outlined in this chapter and in this book.

It is also important to remember that fundraising is not magic. It is a matter of putting good people, with a good cause, into motion. If you can take good processes and put them into motion, a good campaign is a matter of starting at the beginning and working it through to the end. This book contains campaign timelines and checklists to help you make this happen at your nonprofit organization.

The best way to decide how ready you are to embark upon an annual support campaign is to analyze each of the various components outlined within this chapter. Once you have looked at each component and decided if or how well you have achieved it, you will be able to identify your strengths and weaknesses as an organization. The more of the components you have the better. The more complete and confident you are in each component's quality, the better as well. Remember that likely you will never have them all perfectly in place but that the more you have, the more likely you will have success in your endeavors.

Good Campaign Preparations

Good campaign preparation will lead to a good annual campaign effort. The best time to plan for a campaign is before you start rather than waiting until you are heavily involved in doing the campaign. I readily admit that my first annual support campaign was done with little or no preparation and little or any real skill and we still raised a lot of money by our organizational standards at the time. That said, good preparation will lead to a much higher chance of success. By evaluating your abilities and seeing where you have strengths and weaknesses, you can build an annual support campaign that is as strong as it can be. Remember also that your annual support campaign will occur every year. You will have many chances to improve your efforts over the course of many years. Continue to do the hard work of moving your process forward as long as you are not doing damage to your organization through the effort. This means that, generally, as long as you manage your organizational fundraising efforts with integrity, you will have a chance to improve on your efforts as you go along. If you wait for everything to be perfect before starting, you will never begin. So get going!

Factors to Consider Before Starting an Annual Campaign

While you may never have everything in place, you will want to have as much as possible ready before you begin your annual support campaign. An old adage in campaigning is "Ready, Ready, Ready, Ready, Ready, Ready, Aim, Aim, Aim, Aim, Aim, Aim. . . ." At some point, you have to "Fire!" Do not get so intimidated by planning that you never start your campaign. At the same time, rushing an annual support campaign without solid planning efforts would be like starting any other program at your organization without good preparation; its chances for success are hampered at best.

Exercise

Your organization probably has tried to raise charitable funds before, or you may have had some experience with fundraising in the past. Write down the things that caused you challenges or issues in your previous efforts. These could range from time management, to gaining executive buy-in on projects, to issues of volunteer engagement.

1.
2.
3.
4.
5.
6.

Do You Know Who You Are?

While this may seem obvious, it is important for your organization to know who it is, why it exists, and whom it serves. A clear and well-thought-out mission statement is a foundational beginning for your efforts. Ideally, your organization has a mission statement that outlines not only what it strives to do or does but also states how it will affect the lives of those it touches. Active mission statements show and tell the community you serve exactly what it is that you are trying to do. They also leave no room for doubt about who your organization is and what role it plans to play in changing the world.

Do You Have a Strong and Well-Utilized Strategic Plan?

Having an organizational strategic plan that outlines the role that annual support (and other financial development programs, such as capital, endowment, grants, etc.) should play is important in managing and operating your nonprofit. It shows your constituency and your donors that you are thinking clearly and have thought about the ramifications, challenges, and opportunities facing your organization. This strategic plan should outline where your organization is going and how it plans to get there. By having a living, breathing strategic plan—and not one that just sits on the shelf—you give your nonprofit organization the best possible chance of reaching a positive outcome in the months and years ahead. Without a well-organized and well-thought-out strategic plan, your course of action may take you to places that are less than optimal. Another pitfall of not having a specific plan is squandering time and resources through aimless action with no real objectives met.

Exercise

Write down some things about your nonprofit organization that makes you special and unique in your community.

1.
2.
3.
4.
5.
6.

One component of a strong strategic plan should be your organizational financial development plan. This plan should contain details of your entire financial development program including annual, capital, major gifts and endowment issues and goals related to your nonprofit organization. The plan should contain an outline of where you hope to take your annual support campaign this year, next year, and beyond, as well as what you plan to do with the funds raised. This plan would also include details for the annual support campaign, such as volunteer engagement, money raised, donors retained and acquired, and more.

Exercise

If someone gave your organization a very large gift today, what would you do with it? A consistent answer to this question across your organization often shows that a nonprofit truly is worthy of such a gift. What would your organization do with $1 million if it was given today? Write your answer in the space provided.

_____

_____

_____

_____

_____

_____

_____

_____

Now that you have written your response, think about what your top executive would say if asked the same question. What about your top volunteer? What about your board of directors? Would the question elicit the same answer from each person? If not, you must work to create a congruent message about what is truly important to all in your organization. It is important for you to know—as an organization—what it is you want to do with money that is raised. How can you send a clear message about what you are going to do with the money if you do not have internal agreement on how you would spend the money if you raised it? Raising money for your nonprofit will be much more difficult if you do not have internal agreement about these issues.

Are You Doing the Best You Can with the Resources You Have?

Donors want to give to organizations that are good stewards of their funds. By demonstrating to your constituency that a dollar given to you goes a long way and that it is not squandered but invested, you show that you are worthy of charitable support. Spending money wisely and being able to show your constituency that this is the case is fundamental. Whether you show your fiscal responsibility through your governmental reporting forms or through annual reports to donors and constituents, it is a pivotal point. When you can show your community that you are doing the best you can with the resources you have, and that if you only had more, you could truly do more, you are well on your way to a persuasive case for giving.

Make a note to spend quality time understanding how money is raised and spent at your nonprofit organization. Look internally to budget reports and other financial information to share and explain how your organization spends its charitable dollars in the community. By knowing how you spend the money that you already have, you can explain more fully why you are worthy of and deserve additional funding to do even more money to do even more and better work in your community.

Exercise

List individuals in your organization who could help you to more fully understand your nonprofit's finances.

1.
2.
3.
4.
5.
6.

Do You Understand Your Operational Budget?

How your organization spends and earns its money says a great deal about who you are as an organization. There is an old saying that if you want to see what is important to someone, look at where they spend their time and their money. Your organization is no different. It is key for you to be knowledgeable regarding how your organization earns revenue and makes expenditures, so that you can understand why there are gaps, and where they are.

It is extremely important for you to be able to explain to donors and investors why their contributed dollars are needed. If you cannot explain why you need contributed dollars and why they are intrinsic for the success of your organization and the community that it serves, then you should not undertake the activity of fundraising.

Exercise

List some of the largest expenditures in your nonprofit organization. Are your expenses mostly on education? On programming? On overhead?

1.
2.
3.
4.
5.
6.

Once you begin to understand how your nonprofit organization spends its charitable dollars and allocates revenue, it is easier for you to go out and raise funds for your nonprofit.

You are probably doing something to raise money now—perhaps a special event, an annual support campaign, a grant, or something else. Having a concept of how much it costs to raise money in those areas where you are already raising funds is a great first step toward assessing your readiness for annual support. How much did you make on that last special event? How much money did you generate in your last campaign effort? What did it cost you to write and implement that last grant you received? Your organization and the community that you serve deserve to know and understand how much it costs you to raise contributed dollars. If you or your organization are not proud of the amount of money that you are spending to gain contributed income, it should tell you something. If your costs are inordinately high, work toward changing or fixing them. If your costs are low, understand why and share that positive information with your donors and constituency.

Exercise

Once you have looked into and begun to understand your financial information, you can begin to formulate what it really costs you to raise a dollar right now. Think about all of the many things that are involved in raising charitable funds at your organization. List some of those expenses in the blanks that follow. Include things like postage, salaries, and other pertinent costs that you may already be allocating in your nonprofit efforts.

1.
2.
3.
4.
5.
6.

Do You Understand Your Strengths and Weaknesses?

Every organization has both strengths and weaknesses. Your goal and objective in organizing a well-run annual support campaign is to capitalize on your strengths and minimize your weaknesses. What is your organization doing well? What aspects of your organization are particularly strong?

Just as important, what are your weaknesses? Is your board unwilling to engage in fundraising? Do you lack staff experienced in philanthropic endeavors? Your nonprofit organization is only as strong as the programs and services that you offer. Because of this, it is important to know what things you are doing very well and what things you are doing poorly or less well. The next exercises will help you to see these strengths and weaknesses.

Exercise

List some of the specific programs, services, or activities that your organization does particularly well. What are some of the things that you do best?

1.
2.
3.
4.
5.
6.

Exercise

List some of the specific programs, services, or activities that your organization does poorly. What are some of the areas in which you are particularly weak?

1.
2.
3.
4.
5.
6.

Do You Know Who Loves You and Is Willing to Support You?

When you begin to fundraise, it is important to be aware of who in your constituency or community loves and respects you as an organization. Likely there are many people in your midst who greatly appreciate the work that you are doing. These same people may be able to help you financially, or through other means, that can enable you to increase your contributed support. Often people close to the organization can make tremendous differences in the success or failure of your annual support campaign or any of your other financial development efforts.

Exercise

Take a moment to list a few of your most avid fans in the community that you are currently serving. We will return to this topic later in the text, but it is important to begin to think about who cares most for your organization.

1.
2.
3.
4.
5.
6.

Do You Have a Financial Development Plan?

Good planning takes time and initiative. If you are interested in starting or enhancing a fundraising program, then you should be willing to plan and engage your team in the planning process. Outlining the upcoming and current strategy for your annual support campaign is a foundational and necessary step in the overall fundraising process. Taking the time to outline what you will do and when and who will be accountable for each step will ensure that your campaign advances in the right direction.

By putting together a well-outlined plan for how you intend to raise money, you help to ensure that you are maximizing your capabilities and minimizing your weaknesses. Your goal should be to create a plan that states what your goals and objectives are for annual, capital, endowment, and grants for the coming year and years. Be certain that as you create your financial development plan you account for key measures other than just money raised. A common mistake in financial development planning is to think that because you have stated financial development goals in designated areas, your planning is completed. Understanding your needs is really just the beginning. Equally as important are issues that relate to such things as donors acquired and retained.

Having an organized financial development program yields many benefits. Creating an organized financial development program means thinking ahead about the many resources at your disposal, as well as the many issues that you may face as you work towards the goals and objectives that are outlined in your plan. Thinking ahead allows you to decide:

- What fundraising strategies are best for your organization

- How best to utilize your limited financial resources

- How best to utilize your staff resources

- How best to utilize your volunteer resources

- How best to approach your constituency for financial resources

- How best to approach your general community about financial resources

While there are certainly additional things to consider outside of these, this list gives you an idea of why it is so important to truly consider all that you want to accomplish this year (at the very least) with your financial development efforts.

The next example gives one of many reasons why this is so important.

WHY PLANNING IS IMPORTANT

Donors are asked to contribute their time and energy to a special event at your nonprofit organization. They give their time and money to the effort, with much of their money going to underwrite the special event costs for your organization. Three months later (in the same calendar year) you need them to support another fundraising initiative that you have suddenly decided to implement. Your donors are more excited about this initiative than
(continued)

they were your special event but are unable to support or be involved in it because of limited time and financial resources.

In essence, because of your poor planning, you have cheated your donors/volunteers out of a more rewarding giving experience. You have disempowered your donors because you encouraged them to give to a fundraising effort that ultimately proved to be less rewarding for them personally and for the organization. Think of how much more volunteers could give (both with time and money) if each initiative that we asked them to support really spoke to them. They may carve out extra volunteer time from their busy schedule for a program that really strikes a chord with them. Donors and volunteers also may allocate their philanthropic dollars differently if given a broader view.

By planning your overall fundraising for an extended period of time and sharing this information with your donors and volunteers, you enable them to make better choices and to participate more fully. Empower your staff and volunteer team by planning your fundraising and then implementing accordingly.

Do You Have a Board of Directors that Is Passionate (Enough) about Fundraising?

Simply stated, your board needs to be on board with fundraising. A strong board of directors understands that one of its key roles is making sure that the organization has the resources that it needs to fully engage its mission in its community. Most educated boards understand that this means that they need to play a role in fundraising. At this point, many readers are thinking that your board of directors does not do enough with fundraising, and you wish you had a more active board. When it comes to fundraising, the annual support campaign is the effort that most nonprofit organizations will want to grow, develop, and ultimately field test with your board of directors. This campaign is a great time for your board of directors to learn to ask for gifts in addition to going out and telling the story of your organization in the community. If board members are not willing or able to do the work at this level, they will be highly unlikely to help you in major gifts, capital or endowment efforts either.

In my experience, a "spark" on the board with either a single board member or members who see the value in raising charitable support is priceless. Having at least one board member, who is well respected, on the side of good fundraising practice, enables your executive and financial development team to help move the rest of the board towards better fundraising practices. Without at least one board member believing that better fundraising practices are important, you will be hard pressed to make positive changes in your board culture of philanthropy. With one or two enthusiastic and engaged board members, and some focused effort, you can often motivate an otherwise reluctant board to do great work.

Before you recruit members to your board of directors, one of the best things that you can do is to have—and outline—clear expectations for them. This outline explains what you want them to do and how you want and expect them to do it. A thorough job description is a great tool for board members.

Without clear expectations for your board of directors related to fundraising, you will not achieve the best possible results for your philanthropy efforts. This can lead to board members who do not perform to the best of their abilities. You also risk having board members who are disillusioned about what is really expected of them.

Do You Have a Financial Development Committee?

In an ideal world, a nonprofit organization would have a financial development committee charged with advancing philanthropy. This committee would lead volunteer efforts on philanthropic issues related to annual, capital, major gifts, and endowment work. As part of their overall course of work, this volunteer leadership would help to organize around and stimulate growth in the annual support campaign. This committee typically is made up of some board members and some members of your broader community. The financial development committee usually functions as a standing committee of the board of directors, meeting three to four times per year, as needed. It receives its authority from the board, and its actions are subject to review and approval by the board. The committee typically also has the authority to establish ad hoc groups, as necessary, to carry out its work.

TIPS AND TECHNIQUES

Typical Functions of a Financial Development Committee

- Evaluate and recommend financial development strategies inside and outside of the XYZ nonprofit organization's experience to determine which approaches make sense with the mission and culture of the organization and will yield the best results toward accomplishing the strategic goals and objectives of the nonprofit

- Assess the nonprofit's potential for growth in each of the primary areas of financial development—annual giving, capital giving, major gifts and endowment/deferred gifts—and establish short- and long-term objectives for performance.

- Provide the guidance necessary to ensure that nonprofit resources— both financial and human—are utilized appropriately to support goals and objectives of the nonprofit.

- Monitor financial development programs and performance to ensure that the objectives of the nonprofit organization are being met.

- As needed, review proposed financial development policies and recommend their approval by the board of directors.

- Make recommendations regarding the development and cultivation of major gifts from individuals and from corporations, foundations, and other entities as appropriate.

- Identify qualified volunteer leadership needed to achieve financial development goals.

Do You Have a Compelling Reason (Case for Support) to Raise Funds?

Without a compelling reason to need and to raise charitable funds, your nonprofit organization should not be out raising money. Your organization must have genuine and persuasive reasons to require and spend the charitable dollars that it raises each year. Are you expanding the work of your nonprofit? Do you need funding for underwriting critical positions or programming? There are many reasons why your organization may need charitable dollars. If you do not require them, allow other charities to raise the funds in lieu of creating an unimportant purpose. If you do require them as most nonprofits do, then engage volunteers and raise money with the enthusiasm and vigor that you would any noble cause.

Do You Have a Development Budget?

Any development office with a fundraising budget is better off than one without it. A specific budget enables your financial development department to function in a planning and implementation mode rather than in a reactionary mode of operation.. By having a budget, you are able to effectively spend and manage organizational resources to the best of your capabilities. A budget allows you to decide what to spend on each fundraising effort. It also allows you to spread your resources appropriately across all of your fundraising efforts rather than "running out of money" as can often be the case, particularly in smaller organizations. Few things are more frustrating than to plan an important fundraising effort over an extended period of time, only to learn that you cannot put together the funds needed to make it work. Having a development budget that is created and approved by your nonprofit helps to allocate funds on thoughtfully determined efforts rather than haphazardly decided throughout the year.

Are You Afraid to Ask Your Board to Support Your Organization?

Members of your board of directors should recognize and be willing to support your organization through their charitable contributions. Having this understanding in place prior to fundraising efforts will position you much better for success. Why would prospective donors make a contribution if your own board members have not? If the people who are supposed to be the most committed volunteers in your organization are not willing to support it financially, why should others be expected to do so? It is vital, for many reasons, that members of your board of directors understand and acknowledge their role in philanthropy and give generously to the organization relative to their means.

Do You Understand Donor and Prospect Cultivation?

Appreciating that financial development is a process, and one that can sometimes take shorter or longer periods, is important to your overall fundraising efforts. The annual support campaign plays a significant role in the financial development process. Annual support campaigns help donors to realize and comprehend the charitable needs of your organization on a regular basis. Every year, donors and prospects hear about the work that you are doing and are given the opportunity to support it by making a contribution of time and money, or both. The annual support campaign can be the beginning of long-standing and productive relationships for both donors and the organization. We talk more about donor cultivation in Chapter 7, but it is important to understand now that the annual support campaign can be a foundational part of donors truly knowing the work you do and why they should support it.

Do You Know and Are You Willing to Ask Your Base?

The more familiar you are with your constituency, the easier it is to involve them in any programmatic or financial development work that your organization may need accomplished. By being aware of and understanding your donor/member/volunteer base, you are more easily able to identify and build relationships with them. Even when you have substantial relationships with the people who make up your organizational constituency, you still have to find good ways to ask them for their help and support. Knowing your donors and prospects is only part of the effort. You also have to build and implement good systems for asking for their assistance. The annual support campaign can provide this regular and personal giving opportunity to your nonprofit and to your base.

Do You Have a Way to Track and Process Fundraising Information?

Having a system for tracking and processing fundraising-related information helps ensure that you follow laws and utilize data properly for your donors and organization. Without good information systems, important tasks like thank-you letters, gift acknowledgements, report updates, newsletters, and many other aspects of a good donor communications program will not occur. Retaining donors is a fundamental part of annual support and all financial development programs. You certainly don't want a revolving door effect with prospective donors, current donors, or their information. Without good information systems, you will struggle to manage and connect with your donors.

Are You Willing to Rank Your Prospects?

Organizations that analyze their fundraising efforts do better than ones that just do the best they can without assessing their efforts. By looking at your overall donor and prospect listing, you will be better able to see beneficial ways to spend and invest your time and energy. By deciding which prospects are likely to yield the best return on your investment of time and energy, you will help ensure that your efforts produce the most positive and favorable results possible. Prospect ranking can help you determine who should:

- Receive your most personal attention.
- Be asked for the largest gifts.
- Receive the most personalized communications.
- Be telephoned regularly with key updates.
- Receive invitations to key events or friend raisers.
- Other?

By ranking your donors and prospects, you enable your organization to use resources to the best of its ability and earn the highest return on the investment effort. This allows you to provide the best service possible to your donors and to your organization.

Can You Organize Around a Campaign Goal and Objective?

Having good campaign goals and objectives challenges your nonprofit to bring focus, time, and attention to your annual support campaign. Volunteers and staff alike are clear on how and why they are to raise the charitable funds needed to support your key programs or constituency. When volunteers and staff together have a focused understanding of exactly what they are raising money for and exactly where the money will go, they can work most productively and with sincere commitment to achieve the outlined objectives. When volunteers know that, by raising an additional charitable dollar, another child with a disability will go to summer camp or another acre of land will be saved, they are most compelled to work harder and smarter to achieve the goals and objectives outlined in the annual support campaign plan.

Can You Organize a Fundraising Campaign with Appropriate Processes?

Organizing a high-functioning annual support campaign includes things like:

- Planning volunteer recruitment
- Making a calendar
- Generating a timeline
- Writing and updating job descriptions
- Identifying and assigning prospects
- Creating naming opportunities/giving levels
- Reporting back to donors and campaigners

- Determining appropriate campaign management involving staff and volunteers
- Recognizing the work of volunteers
- Other!

To have the best possible annual support campaign, your organization needs to be willing to organize and rally around the campaign. Calendars, job descriptions, and other organizational aspects of a well-run annual support campaign help to ensure that everyone knows what is expected of them and that the annual support campaign stays on track. By organizing around a comprehensive annual support campaign plan, the entire campaign team can be assured that the best possible outcome will be ultimately achieved.

Are You Willing to Recruit Others to Help You Fundraise?

Some organizations believe that staff should do all of the work and volunteers should be involved only in setting policy and acting as figureheads. Often volunteers in these organizations remain in board posts for decades and perform little in terms of real work. While they may enjoy many chicken dinners over the years, these volunteers often go underutilized and divide their time among many different boards with little fruitful engagement. Does this sound like your board of directors?

If this sounds like your board of directors, then you may have a challenge in asking volunteers to do the work that is fundraising within your organization. These challenges likely come from many possible reasons including:

- Fear and anxiety on the part of the board or the management team or both
- Concern that board members will turn you down if you ask them to do real work
- An existing culture that says volunteers do not do this type of work
- An executive who does not clearly outline expectations for board members, which include fundraising and financial development work

- Financial development staff members who believe that they can or should do it all alone

- A board that believes that the staff should raise the money—"that is what we pay them for . . ."

- A belief that only staff can make good asks for funds as volunteers lack the professional abilities or skills to do it well

- Concerns over training or fully explaining the mission to your volunteers

- Other?!

You could come up with almost countless reasons why your organization might struggle with the concept of engaging volunteers in the work of fundraising. If you are willing to ask and recruit volunteers, and if you give them the support tools they need to do the job well, I promise you that you will have some very pleasant surprises in your fundraising efforts.

 IN THE REAL WORLD

I worked with an annual support campaign that was operated as part of a human services organization that had been in existence for over 100 years. Although the nonprofit had only been doing an annual support campaign for about 10 years, it had built a deep culture of performance and success with its volunteer workforce. With over 1,000 volunteers now actively involved and engaged in the work of telling the story of this organization in the community and then asking for money, the volunteer force had become a seasoned and high-functioning arm of the organization. Each year this group of dedicated volunteers helped raise over $3 million by doing what some would consider to be staff work.

The relationships that these individuals brought to the organization, and the passion that they brought to the work, were priceless. It made friends, raised funds, and invigorated the staff as well. There was true momentum here and the benefits far outweighed any investment of energy, time, or resources that were put toward volunteer development.

One year this same human services organization decided to do a capital campaign to raise funds for increased facilities. In the capital campaign effort, there were four, and only four, gifts made to the organization; each was over $1 million. Each gift had four things in common:

1. The individual giving the gift was a past chair of the annual support campaign.

2. Each individual had given at least $25,000 to the annual campaign in the previous year.

3. When the capital campaign came around, these committed donors continued to give their $25,000 annual campaign pledge and, in addition, gave a five-year pledge of at least $1,000,000 to the capital campaign.

4. Each donor had been a long-term volunteer in the annual support campaign.

These donors were undeniably financially well off, but the point remains the same: They had become a strong and functioning part of a culture of philanthropic organizational support. Also, each of these individuals had very deep involvement as a fundraising volunteer in the annual support campaign.

There may be many reasons why these individuals stood out among the rest, but here are a few reasons why I believe they made these large gifts. These supporters:

- Fully understood the mission of the organization.

- Knew the story of the organization as if it were their own—because it was their own.

- Had strong passion and commitment to the organization.

- Had developed a habit of giving to the organization.

- Had long-term relationships with the organization.

- Developed long- and short-term trust with the organization.

- Had seen that the organization was a good steward of the funds that it received.

- Other?!

Likely there were many reasons why these donors gave their gifts, but I am confident that without the annual support campaign, these gifts would not have been obtained as readily nor would they have been as large. The annual support campaign helps your nonprofit organization develop its community and volunteers in many ways.

Are You Willing to Solicit Charitable Funds in Your Community?

In order for you to raise money, you have to be willing to go out and ask for it. While this may seem obvious, if you are not truly willing to go out and ask, the funds are unlikely to just appear. I have worked, as a consultant, with fabulous nonprofit professionals who had years of service and relationships in organizations, but had no practice or understanding of the missing component in their effort. They didn't have a high functioning annual campaign every year, which would have given them the opportunity to ask, and they didn't realize how much philanthropic funding they were missing out on. When these professionals finally went to their constituents to actually ask for money, they were often surprised that their constituents were more than eager to give their funds. You must be willing to ask. You also must acknowledge and accept the necessary work that it will take to organize and involve both volunteers and staff in this fundraising effort, since it is most definitely a team effort.

Do You Have an Attitude of Success and Believe that You Can and Will Succeed?

You have to believe that you can have a successful annual support campaign, and you have to be able to convey that belief to others. Without the belief that you can succeed in an annual campaign, your ability to raise charitable dollars will be greatly hindered. Without confidence, you will struggle the first time you come to an obstacle or a difficult situation—and you will much more likely fail. Believe in the fact that this method of campaigning has been done literally thousands of times in different places and that it will work for you as well. Remember that each annual support campaign you run will get better as your organization continues to learn and grow.

Do You Have Staff in Place to Track and Manage Campaign-Related Information?

No matter the size of your nonprofit organization, you must have a comprehensive system and process in place to monitor and track campaign-related information. Staff typically organize and maintain this data. It is important to record both the revenues and expenses of any fundraising effort in order to have a complete picture. The data that you collect will be vital for use during and after a campaign, and will lay a solid foundation for future annual support campaigns. Some of the many items that you will want to be able to track and account for include:

- Money deposits
- Pledge entries
- Gift entries
- Data entries
- Data management
- Gift acknowledgments
- Individual campaigner money tracking
- Individual goals
- Team goals
- Campaign expenses
- How the money is ultimately spent within your organization
- Other!

There are many things to document in an annual support campaign but this list gives you a basic start. The idea is to keep track of data so when it comes time to explain—to anyone who asks—what happened and why the campaign results are what they are, everyone can understand and be proud of the ultimate results. Further, these records will allow you to improve each year if you use them as evaluation tools, planning guides and starting points for future annual campaigns. More on this topic is covered in Chapter 8.

Can You Teach People How to Fundraise with Best Practices?

Fundraising and the financial development process are skills that are learned and acquired through education and practice. It is essential to be willing to work with both staff and volunteers as they learn to fundraise properly and with the best possible practices. Taking the time and energy to work with individuals as they build personal confidence in their fundraising capabilities is a crucial part of the fundraising process. One of the best things about an annual support campaign is that it gives people the opportunity to practice fundraising every year. By enabling individuals to learn and enhance their skills annually, over time you will build an extremely capable fundraising force. This workforce becomes a powerful advocate team for your nonprofit organization, in addition to helping you raise significant funds. By training and working with staff and volunteers, you are investing in the future of your nonprofit and your nonprofit's fundraising efforts. By training your staff and volunteers on effective fundraising practices, you help to grow your organization and spread the message of the great work that you are doing, in the most productive way possible.

Can You Steward Gifts Appropriately?

When you begin an annual support campaign, you must understand the obligation of being a good steward of your donors, your prospects, your gifts, and the funds that you raise. When people give you money to benefit the good cause that you are working on, they are giving you a sacred trust that should be taken very seriously. Think of all the work that went into making this gift happen! When you consider it, each gift to a nonprofit is a treasure that should be spent wisely and thanked profusely. When you take the time to think about it, a lot of effort likely went into making each and every one of our charitable gifts happen. Someone cared enough about your organization to make a gift. That may have been the result of years of caring about your organization. It may have been the result of a staff member or volunteer making a connection with the person and then making a personal ask. It may have been the result of carefully designed and worded campaign materials that were reviewed with a loved one. It may have been the result of a colleague sharing passion for the organization. It may have been the result of a lifetime's worth of involvement that is culminating in a gift laden with memories. To be sure it was pennies earned by someone, which turned into dollars. When you look at all of the time that it may have taken to get that charitable gift, it is easy to recognize just how much we should appreciate both the donor and the gift. Too many nonprofit organizations take both the gifts that they received and the donors who made the gifts for granted. When you take the time to reflect on how a gift was ultimately made to your nonprofit organization, it is clear that taking the time to be a diligent steward of those donors and gifts is a truly wise investment.

Many guides and books tell you to be a good steward of gifts and donors because it is the right thing to do philosophically. Someone was nice to you; therefore, you should show kindness and thanks in return. Although this certainly is true, to do otherwise is really bad business practice as well. A lot of effort and resources went into getting a charitable gift; making sure that donors feel and know that they are appreciated is valuable from the perspective of keeping your customer. Being a responsible steward of funds is not only the right thing to do, it is just good business.

Are You Willing To Create and Manage Accurate Office Systems?

The best development programs and indeed the best annual support campaigns rely heavily on the confidentiality and accuracy of business office systems. Although you do not necessarily need the latest or greatest software programs, it helps to have reliable and accurate data systems as well as responsible personnel to manage or interface with them. I will take a trustworthy, detail-oriented person over the most reliable software any day as the data is only as good as the person who is managing it. Work hard to make sure that your organization has the software that it needs and, even more importantly, make sure that your organization has a dependable, retainable staff member to help you manage the information. Without an individual whose job it is to monitor and carefully enter key donor information, your financial development program will be doomed before it begins. Do not use this as an excuse not to proceed. Do use it as an excuse to put resources into this area of your financial development department.

Consider these questions, among others, when working with or choosing a technology system:

- Does it integrate well with other software in the office? Having multiple databases can cause problems or challenges with donor and prospect mailing or contact information.

- Can it generate the reports you need related to last year's donors and this year's prospects? You will want to be able to sort and differentiate this information relative easily.

- Can you learn and use the software properly? Many organizations buy powerful software only to use its simplest applications. Make sure that you buy software that can grow with you but that you can start using today.

- Can you generate collection and contribution-related reports?

- Can you track donor and prospect information as you need to, including resolving issues such as matching and restricted gifts?

- Can you generate pledge statements and reminder letters directly from the database itself?

- Can you adequately meet issues related to donor ethics and confidentiality? (These topics are covered in the appendix of this text.) Some examples of these issues include donor privacy, recognition, and mailing lists.

- Can you differentiate among your various fundraising campaigns (annual, capital, endowment, special events, grants, etc.)?

These are just a few of the many issues that you will need to resolve before choosing donor software. I have worked with organizations utilizing software programs from Microsoft Excel, to Donor2, to Blackbaud Raisers Edge. Remember that "garbage in equals garbage out" and that the most overriding piece of any fundraising database is the people doing the entry work. Without adequate training and investment in the human resource aspects of software, you will not get the results that you need to maintain a high-level development program and annual support campaign.

Are You Willing to Cultivate Gifts Appropriately?

Central to all financial development work, including annual support campaign work, is the tenet that you are willing to talk to and stay in touch with donors and prospects, even when you are not asking them for a gift. Many nonprofit organizations make the mistake of talking to their donors only when they are making a solicitation. It is no wonder that some donors feel like little more than automatic teller machines (ATM) that distribute funds when their buttons are pushed. It is important to have a communications program that ensures that you stay in touch with donors between solicitations so that they know how money is being utilized and also how your organization is doing. By being willing to communicate with donors in more and less personal ways between solicitations and annual support campaigns, you will build deep relationships with your donors over time. This investment of positive human energy can lead people to give more time to your organization—and larger gifts as well. This is in addition to the rewarding personal and professional relationships that will be built through this worthy process.

Can You Put Together Appropriate Materials for a Campaign?

Support materials must be created and compiled in order for your annual support campaign to be effective. Pieces like campaigner training materials, pledge cards, case statement information (where your organization tells why it is raising money and why it needs the funds), frequently asked questions information, and other literature not only help staff and volunteers understand what it is that you are trying to do; these pieces also make sure that your story is being communicated consistently in your community. By putting together campaign materials that explain what you are doing and how people can support your work, you are making sure that everyone has the best campaign information possible.

A donor wants to make a big gift. Can she pay by credit card? If so, what kind? What is your Web site address for more information? Has it been updated to represent your organization well? What about the other sources of funding that your organization receives? If a person already has made a gift of some kind to your organization this year, does it count toward your donor recognition levels? How is the money being spent? Where is the money going? These types of information are extremely helpful to staff members or volunteers as they work to explain your efforts to prospective or existing donors. By taking the time to answer these questions in appropriate informational materials that are easy to use by staff and volunteers, you help to make the campaign easier for everyone to implement and manage.

Do You Have a Communications Plan?

A major role of the annual support campaign is communicating your mission to the staff, to the volunteers, to the public, and to your constituency about the fact that you are a charitable organization. I regularly work with nonprofit organizations that the public does not even know are nonprofits! Imagine that it is the end of the year, and someone is considering making a gift to a charitable organization. If the public does not know that you are a charity, they will never think of you. That would be a tragedy for you, your organization, and your constituency. A well-run annual support campaign shares your organizational story with all who come into contact with it.

Volunteers and staff alike share the stirring and poignant stories that make your nonprofit special. With a well-honed communications plan, the true story of impact is told in your community. Donors and prospects can evaluate your mission and your work and choose to support it accordingly. The value of this work is shown not only in the dollars raised through your annual support campaign but also in the friends and community that are built through the efforts. This public relations and marketing benefit can be priceless when replicated year after year in your community.

TIPS AND TECHNIQUES

Developing a Communications Plan

- What are your goals and objectives?
  a. Make sure to state what you are trying to accomplish in clear and easy-to-understand language. Everyone on your fundraising team should be able to understand everything in your communications plan, including your mission statement, what you are trying to do, and whom you are trying to affect.
  c. Make sure that you can do what you say you are going to do, with the resources you have available to you. Understand your strengths and weaknesses. Work to focus on your strengths and get help with your weaknesses.

- Who do you wish you could serve or what do you wish you could do that you currently cannot? Also, consider sharing with donors what you wish you could do if you had the charitable funds that you really require to complete or more fully fulfill your mission.

- Who are your potential funding sources? What does the audience that you are communicating to look for in communication plans? Is there anyone else who might be interested in what you are doing or trying to do? Make sure that you understand the marketplace for your mission, your goals, and your objectives. Try to explain how you are different without disparaging others.

- What are your key messages? Does everyone on your staff and volunteer team agree on the key messages?

(continued)

a. Can your staff and volunteer teams articulate what it is that you are trying to achieve? Ideally, everyone states the same case in their own personalized way, resulting in a host of great "elevator speeches" that share the spirit and the specifics of what you are trying to accomplish.

c. In this communication effort, what do you want people to focus on most about you, and how can you emphasize that? What do you want people to do with the information once they have learned it? How will you communicate this information?

- Are you truly working together on your communications with both the staff and the volunteers of the organization?

- Does your staff know what speaks to your volunteers? Does your board know what key leadership staff members are thinking? Is your marketing group working in a vacuum? Everyone should be on the same page when it comes to communications regarding your fund-raising program. When board, staff, key volunteers, and major donors are all stating that the same things are important, you know that you are ready for a strong campaign.

- 'Once you have the communications plan, how will you evaluate its success? Are there realistic and measurable goals in place to evaluate the success of this effort? Are your objectives able to be acted on and altered if things do not go as you hope or expect? Think through how you will know if this aspect of your program works or needs fixing.

Can You Hold Appropriate Campaign-Related Meetings?

Campaign-related meetings are very worthwhile as we work to communicate all of the information that we have to share around an annual support campaign. Time together can do a lot to build energy and momentum around your cause, in addition to giving people the opportunity to belong to something that is bigger than themselves. Campaign meetings offer the setting to train your campaigners on things such as how to ask for a gift, share timely campaign updates, and inspire volunteers by hearing testimonials of people served by the funds raised. These meetings also bring people together around the effort that is your annual support campaign. By building this community and using people's time wisely, you will create a more educated team of staff and volunteers as well as develop increased loyalty and participation in your fundraising process. There are many ways to provide coaching sessions (also called training or orientation sessions), campaign kickoffs, reports, celebrations, and victories. A few things are important to remember as you plan and hold campaign meetings.

Meetings should be:

- *Time sensitive.* Use people's time wisely!

- *Personal.* Both the volunteer and staff member are important to your nonprofit. Show them that you really care by making these meetings as personal as possible.

- *Informational.* What we are doing and how we are doing it.

- *Promotional.* This is great work that is making a difference.

- *Explanatory.* Why do we do what we do.

- *Rewarding.* You want to do this again and again because it is rewarding and fun.

- *Networking.* People should have the opportunity to get to meet and know others who are committed to this campaign.

- *Other?*

Recognize that Timing Can Be Critical

One factor that can be difficult for organizations to determine is when to have an annual support campaign, especially if it is for the first time. Previously in the text I stated that the best time to fundraise is when you are ready. This remains true. Other factors to consider for annual support campaigns are:

- *Your market.* What else is happening in your community? Are there other annual support campaigns of note occurring around the same time frame, such as United Way or Earth Share? Does that matter to your organization's potential success?

- *Your constituency.* Does a certain time of year make more sense for your donor base? Don't forget to consider holidays and other distractions that might divide your donor's time, attention, or money.

- *Other fundraising efforts.* Are you raising money in major gift, capital or endowment efforts? If you are, you still will want to have an annual support campaign, but there may be a logical way to integrate the concept for your donor base.

- *Your board calendar.* When are logical times to have board members actively engaged, as appropriate? What else are you asking your board members to do this year, and on what schedule?

- *Your staff calendar.* What programs take the most time and energy for staff to manage and operate? When is a time of year that staff can give more attention to making the campaign run smoothly?

- *Other volunteer commitments.* Key volunteers can make or break an annual support campaign. If it is your first year, it also makes sense for you to consider the schedules of key volunteers.

Although there are many things to consider when looking at the timing of an annual support campaign, the most compelling factor to consider is when you are ready. People will give you lots of reasons why it is not the best time to fundraise, but when you can muster the strength, courage, and conviction to undertake the annual support campaign, it just may be the right time in your calendar to make it happen.

You Have a Willing and Capable Staff Member

Remember from Chapter 1 that there are four components to a successful annual support campaign: staff component, board component, major gifts component, and community gifts component. Having a willing staff member who can devote the time and energy to the necessary tasks behind the operation of an annual campaign is ideal. In many smaller nonprofit organizations, this person is the executive director, perhaps with the help of an administrative support person. In nonprofit organizations with no staff at all, a willing volunteer can serve this purpose. In this text, however, we will assume that your nonprofit organization has staff members and that, a staff member will lead the campaign from a staff perspective. This staff person serves as campaign director, not campaign chair. The chair should always be a volunteer.

Are You Willing to Commit to a Postcampaign Evaluation of Your Efforts and Learn From It?

The best thing about annual support campaigns is that they occur every year. The annual support campaign provides a consistent learning laboratory for your nonprofit about everything from brand messaging to what your donors are really thinking. But this is true only if you are willing to listen and learn. Performing a postcampaign evaluation allows you to determine what worked and what did not. It allows you to see which communications resonated with your volunteers, staff, and donors, and it allows you to fix mistakes for the next year. It makes sure that your efforts are as good as they can be . . . for your donors, your constituency, and the next annual support campaign. You should follow every annual support campaign with an evaluation to see what you did well and what you could do better. There is more about campaign evaluation in Chapter 8.

Summary

Your organization can do many things to get geared up and fully prepared for an annual support campaign. Remember that the best time to fundraise is when your organization is ready. However, work hard not to create excuses for your organization not to raise charitable funds. It is all too easy to say that you are not ready rather than to take the sometimes frightening step to go out and raise the money needed to accomplish your nonprofit organization's charitable objectives.

Being as prepared as you can be this year to do an annual support campaign just makes good sense. As you can see from this chapter, there are lots of issues and challenges that may be worthy of your time and attention in order for your organization to be as ready as it can be to do annual support. Knowing and working on the many aspects of effective fundraising will help you in becoming more prepared to embark on your annual support campaign effort.

With that said, do everything possible not to become overwhelmed by all that this chapter had to say about campaign readiness. The list is intentionally long as it gives a comprehensive view of a highly developed fundraising processes. The more well defined answers we can give our donors and prospective donors, the more that they will understand the important work that we are doing in our community and also be willing to support it. At the same time, people who know you and love you will be often willing to support you in spite of your flaws. This is no excuse, however, for not doing our preparation work as well as we are capable of doing it.

It is my hope that you can and will muster the courage to undertake an annual support campaign at your organization—this year! Do not wait for everything to be perfect or for everyone to be ready before undertaking your annual support campaign effort. Do, however, take the time to compile and review key information, then plan and strategize before undertaking the effort. By so doing, you will be rewarded with the best possible annual support campaign effort possible. Begin where is reasonable for your organization, and commit to making each year's annual support campaign a little better!

Developing the Case for Support

After reading this chapter, you will be able to:

- Understand the importance and identify the components of a well-developed case for giving.
- Define your case for support and its key factors.
- Develop a case for support for your own nonprofit organization.

A cornerstone for your annual support campaign is a well- thought-out case for support. A case for support is the synthesized story of what your organization is doing and why it needs the support of its donors. It is often portrayed in the written materials that are created to encapsulate the key messages of the campaign, but it is also reflected in the words and phrases that are used by staff and volunteers. It is the reason and set of facts utilized to "make the case" for your annual support campaign.

A strong case is almost always best achieved by involving key groups of staff and volunteers in the process. By outlining your annual campaign case with this broad group, you can solicit participation and buy-in from all regarding the important undertaking that is the annual campaign. Further, a willing team will be able to collaborate and brainstorm toward a better final product and overall message. By engaging people in the conversations about what it is you are trying to do and what you are going to raise the money for, you are also taking a major first step toward actually raising the funds.

Case statement examples are interspersed throughout the chapter to add a depth and breadth to the topic of nonprofit annual campaign case statements. These pieces are included to show you how others have defined and explained their case for support to their broader communities. There are almost countless additional examples of annual campaign case statements on the Internet of nonprofit organizations from around the world. Look at each example throughout the chapter or on the Web to determine what makes each unique and impactful. Would you give one of these organizations a gift? Think about what makes each case for giving compelling in terms of it motivating you personally to make a gift.

In order to determine why someone should want to invest in your nonprofit organization's annual support campaign (or any other campaign, for that matter), it is necessary to think through and address the many different questions, concerns and issues that may arise. The next section focuses on key areas your organization should consider as you work through and develop your annual support campaign case for support.

Developing the Case for Annual Support

What Issues are Facing Your Community?

You have a mission that you are focusing on as an organization. What issues are your community dealing with right now that are congruent with your mission objectives? The answers are likely as close as your community blog or news headline. Your annual support campaign should consider addressing one or more of these key issues faced by your constituency. Whether you are a shelter for battered women or a food bank feeding the hungry, you must show that the money being raised through your annual support campaign will be well used to

One gift.
Every year.
Any amount.

Impact of **Support**

- Undergraduate scholarships
- Graduate fellowships
- Campus programs and initiatives
- Maintaining and developing outreach programs
- Campus computer hardware and software
- Hiring of the best and brightest faculty

UC Irvine is recognized as one of the nation's best public universities (*U.S. News & World Report*). Those rankings are based, in part, on strong alumni participation. Private support through annual gifts is the primary factor in establishing the alumni participation rate that is often used to leverage additional support from state and federal offices and plays a role in rankings. The higher the participation rate, the higher UC Irvine's national rankings. The higher UC Irvine's ranking, the more valuable your degree.

To learn about UCI's Shaping the Future campaign, please visit:
www.ucifuture.com

University of California, Irvine
Office of Annual Giving
4199 Campus Drive, Suite 400
Irvine, CA 92697-5601
949-824-7932
annualfund@uci.edu
www.egiving.uci.edu

Matching **Gift Program**

Many employers sponsor matching gift programs and will match any charitable contributions made by their employees. If your company offers this type of program, your gift to UC Irvine can be doubled or tripled!

To determine if your company matches gifts supporting higher education, contact your human resources or payroll office. You also may visit www.matchinggifts.com for a complete list of companies that offer matching gift programs.

"You make a living by what you get.
You make a life by what you give."
— Winston Churchill

GIVING TO
UC IRVINE

We live in challenging times, but challenges must not overwhelm hope, and solutions can be found. That's what great universities do.

As a state-assisted (not state-supported) institution, the University of California, Irvine receives approximately 15 percent of its budget from state appropriations. Private giving, together with state allocations, tuition revenue and endowment income, must make up the majority of UC Irvine's current budget.

As support from state and federal sources decreases, private support from alumni, friends, parents and students plays an increasingly significant role in enhancing the quality of the university.

Your support provides more than simply "extras" not available through other sources of funding ... it is critical for advancing UC Irvine.

Your gift translates into student scholarships, faculty awards, new equipment for class-rooms, support for libraries and countless other important needs. In many cases, your contributions provide educational opportunities that otherwise would not be available.

UC Irvine's Office of Annual Giving is an integral partner to the campus in its efforts of preserving the quality of education that UC Irvine strives to provide for today's Anteaters.

We need your help to take on today's toughest challenges. We've learned that

hard work by bright and caring people greatly benefits our community and our state. Their hard work also produces valuable new products and services that boost our economy.

The Office of Annual Giving is a key campus partner that helps enhance the quality of education for today's Anteaters.

THE UCI FUND

The UCI Fund provides unrestricted funds to support the growth and needs of the university. These unrestricted dollars are primarily used to fund scholarships, fellowships and other priorities designated by the Chancellor.

SCHOOL
CAMPAIGN

The School Campaign provides annual support for the developing needs of each of UC Irvine's outstanding schools. You have the opportunity to earmark your support to any school, department or program within the university. Approximately 63 percent of the gifts received each year are directed by donors to support programs of personal interest.

HOW TO GIVE

Gifts can be made three ways:

PHONE

UC Irvine student callers contact alumni, parents and friends to inform them of UC Irvine's progress. During this call, you may choose to make a gift to the UCI Fund or to a specific school on campus. If you have not received a phone call from a student and would like to make a gift to UCI, you may call: (949) 824-7932.

MAIL

More than 6,000 campus friends make gifts every year via mail by responding to letters mailed throughout the year that include a detachable pledge card.

Gifts also can be mailed at anytime to:

University of California, Irvine
Office of Annual Giving
4199 Campus Drive, Suite 400
Irvine, CA 92697-5601

ONLINE

Giving online is fast, convenient and eco-friendly. Gifts of any size to any program can be made with a credit card. Visit www.egiving.uci.edu 24 hours a day to make your gift. Installment options also are available.

I would like to show my support to the UCI Fund: ☐

Please charge my ☐ Visa ☐ MasterCard ☐ Discover ☐ American Express

for a gift of: ☐ $500 ☐ $250 ☐ $100 ☐ Other $ _____

Credit Card # _____ Exp. _____

Signature _____

Enclosed is a gift of: ☐ $500 ☐ $250 ☐ $100 ☐ Other $ _____

Please make checks payable to: *The UCI Foundation*

Stay in touch by updating your contact info:

Address: _____

City/State/ZIP: _____

E-mail: _____

The information you provide will be used for University business and will not be released unless required by law. A portion of all gifts are used to defray the costs of administering the funds. All gifts are tax-deductible as prescribed by law.

address an important community issue. In many ways, the more urgent or regularly occurring the need, the better it is for your case, since an annual support campaign happens every year. When your organization shows that it has financial needs that must be addressed every year, it helps to educate and convince your donor and prospect population to the crucial work of your organization.

Exercise

Take a moment to write down some larger issues facing your community now that your nonprofit organization is involved in helping with or could be helping to improve.

1.
2.
3.
4.
5.
6.

How Is Your Nonprofit Organization Responding to Important Community Issues?

It is not enough to know that there are needs; it is essential that our nonprofit organizations are taking action to make positive changes towards rectifying these issues. In your case for support, you want to outline how your nonprofit organization is taking action to make the world a better place. Show how, if someone gives you funds for your annual support campaign, they are actually providing solid options for more at-risk youth in your city or town. Show that if someone gives you money, more people can be helped in times of natural disasters. Show that if you raise another dollar in contributed income, you will be able to save another endangered animal from becoming extinct. Whatever your mission and cause is, it is critical to represent how, if someone gives you money, a correlating positive change will occur.

Exercise

Take a moment now to write down how your organization is responding or could respond to these issues in your community.

1.
2.
3.
4.
5.
6.

How Will This Campaign Change the World?

Most nonprofit organizations try to have mission statements and visions that clearly outline how they propose to change the world through their work and actions. Ideally, your annual support campaign is no different from any of the other key work that you are doing in your community. Bottom line, your annual support campaign should be a natural and logical extension of the vital work that you are already doing to serve your constituency.

When you examine your mission statement, you will likely see clues as to what will make for a strong case for annual support. If you look closely, phrases like "Help people to achieve" or "Protect the environment so that" or "Build

---

Exercise

List the ways that someone can change your community for the better by giving to your nonprofit's annual support campaign.

1.
2.
3.
4.
5.
6.

---

strong communities" all show action toward improving the efforts of the communities served by our nonprofit organizations. The annual support campaign should be an expansion of your normal programming efforts.

Are You Making Lasting Change Through Your Organizational Efforts?

How does the annual support campaign help you to make lasting change? By addressing the idea that, over time, positive change can occur, you are helping people to understand that your mission is not necessarily one that will be achieved in one year and then be complete. Indigent patients need healthcare assistance every year. People with disabilities need life-improving programs every year. Recovering substance abusers need rehabilitation programs every year. Child advocacy programs need professionals to represent children every year. People in crisis need hotlines or centers to be available every year. By showing that you are working on an annual need but addressing a longer-term issue, you can help people to see the value of your efforts on a longer-term basis as well. You are beginning to make the case as to why you will be coming back to them to ask again next year. Your constituency's education both begins and continues with this valuable work!

By outlining how you make lasting change, you construct yet another argument for the importance of your work in the nonprofit sector. One example of this is the student who receives a scholarship from a college or university. Proof of the merits of the value of college scholarships may be to show hard data on how students who graduate from college earn more than their high school graduate peers. By showing the value of a college education, you can then make the argument that donors who give to an annual support campaign to fund college scholarships for those who could not otherwise afford college help lift someone out of a possible negative economic circumstance and into a better one. You could then show how college graduates eventually contribute to society in a more active or involved way. You could also show how students who are engaged in this scholarship program at your college make substantial change through their service to the community because of their engagement in the university that has now given them so much. There are countless ways to show that giving to your annual support campaign might make profound change in the community that you serve.

Exercise

List the fundamental changes in your community that could occur by someone making a gift to the annual support campaign. How would the world be changed through the noteworthy work that you are doing?

1.

2.

3.

4.

5.

6.

What Programs and Services Will Receive Funding?

It is important that you explain to your prospects and donors exactly what you plan to do with the money that you are raising through your annual support campaign.. This is a great time to explain all of the great work that you are doing that perhaps the public knows little or nothing about. Often programs or services that are heavily subsidized at our organizations are not well marketed or explained to the community at large. In other instances, you may want to expand an existing program that is going well. Perhaps you would like to reduce your reliance on government funding or grants that may or may not be available in the future. Take the time in your annual support campaign case for support to tell your community about the tremendous programs that you are doing where these funds are critically needed. Talk about what makes your programs more effective and so needed. Discuss the things that make your organization special that are related to raising these necessary funds from your annual support campaign.

Exercise

List specific programs and services offered at your nonprofit organization that could be helped through an annual support campaign.

1.
2.
3.
4.
5.
6.

What New Programs Might Annual Campaign Funding Support?

If your organization needs or wants to begin a new program, the annual campaign can offer a possible funding solution. The case for support may actually be a very good way to introduce new or additional programs to your public. In these cases, make sure to provide a clear explanation about why the program is important and how it will make a difference in your community.

Be mindful, however, that whatever programs you start, run, or operate will need continuing support year after year. While this can make a stronger case for future annual campaigns, there are obviously increased challenges to consider. New programs will mean increased management demands and long term funding solutions. The program or service that you will be delivering, may be able to be entirely funded through the annual campaign, or may need additional funding. As well, take care to add programs that have been carefully considered from all angles and perspectives. Potential donors want to know that their money is funding a program or service that has been well thought out.

Exercise

List some possible programs and services that you could offer at your non-profit organization if you had the annual income generated by an annual support campaign.

1.

2.

3.

4.

5.

6.

How Will These Funds Improve Your Community?

Get to the heart of what you are trying to do with this money. Talk about how the world will be a better place if people give you their hard-earned funds. Will some part of the world be changed? If so, how? By showing how people's money can truly make a difference in your community, you give donors the opportunity to make positive community change through your organization. In order for most people to contribute, they must be aware and believe that they can help make these great changes happen and that your organization can help them to accomplish these efforts.

Exercise

List the ways that your community will be truly changed through someone giving to your annual support campaign.

1.

2.

3.

4.

5.

6.

How Has Your Organization Already Changed the World?

In your campaign case, enlighten your community about how your organization is already making an impact. By explaining what you do, you prove to people who may be willing to support your efforts that you can do great things. By showing people that your work is effective, you illustrate to them that you are worthy of additional charitable gift funding. This makes asking for additional funding a logical next step.

Also, consider showing how many children, animals, students, adults—whatever—you have already helped. Outline all of the many ways that your work has benefitted the community, and make sure to consider including any relevant explanations about numbers served or lives changed. This kind of data, in an easy-to-grasp format, coupled with the rest of the campaign case, can be very motivating information for donors and prospects.

Exercise

Take a moment to outline some of the many ways that your important work has already made the world a better place.

1.
2.
3.
4.
5.
6.

Why Do You Need the Money Now?

What will not happen if you do not get the money you need in the annual support campaign? Whose lives will *not* be changed if you do not get these desperately needed funds? Describe the improvements that can happen, and then detail how things might not change at all if you do not raise the money that your organization needs. By explaining the change that you can make now, you provide donors with the opportunity to participate in making the change happen with you. That can make people feel involved and inspired!

Exercise

Write down some of the many reasons why you need the money now. For example, if you do not get money to send children to summer camp, these children will spend an unsupervised summer at home or on the street.

1.

2.

3.

4.

5.

6.

Why Are You the Best Organization to Do This Work?

Are there other organizations that do what you do? If so, how are you different? By demonstrating how your programs are successful or fulfilling a niche, you give donors the inside view on how your programs serve people or your community in a unique way. Be sure not to denigrate other nonprofit or for-profit groups, but do show potential supporters how your organization and programs are special. Remember the community may not know that much, if anything, about your organization, so take this chance to share your mission and let it shine!

When you write or speak about how you are the best organization to do the projects for which you are raising funds in your annual support campaign, use words and phrases that share key facts that will resonate with prospective donors. What statistics or meaningful data can you share? Information that explains how many people are going to be helped or what new state-of-the-art technology can be purchased that will help save lives

---

Exercise

Write down some of the many ways in which your organization is different from others in your marketplace or in your community. What is unique about how your organization addresses the issues and challenges it faces?

1.
2.
3.
4.
5.
6.

---

helps donors see how their funds directly affect your critical mission work. You want people to clearly understand why they should give you one more dollar to help one more person or help resolve one more issue. You want people to understand that because *you* have done this work a long time or because *you* have extremely experienced staff people or because *you* really do understand the issues and have a passion for them . . . that it is *your* organization that can really make the difference. These points likely will resonate with your prospective donors, and you are more likely to get their contributed support.

Exercise

Why is your organization the best one to perform these programs and services in your community? List some of the reasons here.

1.
2.
3.
4.
5.
6.

Do You Have Stories that Explain Your Work with Passion?

At the same time you are listing facts, consider including in your case for giving, compelling examples that show what it is that you are accomplishing and why you are trying to accomplish it. A story of inspiring children or the downtrodden can be an extremely powerful part of a case for support. By using emotion in appropriate ways, you can help donors to feel that, even more than helping a certain number of people or things, your organization is really transforming lives. Sharing a real life example also gives the reader insights which can take it from a general issue to a personal one. When we read about a young woman who was homeless and got into Harvard, or about the refugee from a war-torn country who has become a highly successful part of our community, we realize that someone or something helped them along the way. These stories can evoke emotions that catapult supporters to participate more fully in an annual support campaign.

Exercise

List some possible stories within your nonprofit organization. If you know of specific stories that are powerful, list them here. If you do not know specific emotionally powerful stories regarding your nonprofit, list people or places where you might find them.

1.
2.
3.
4.
5.
6.

Does Your Case Appeal to People's Hearts and Minds?

Some people think of the overall case for support as a combination of connecting with the "head" and the "heart" of your donors and prospects. The "head" is the fact-based aspect of the case statement that outlines the important facts and figures that people would want to know about your programs and campaign. The "heart" is the emotional appeal that focuses on stories, images, or feelings to make the points necessary to motivate a charitable gift. When you can marry these two very different aspects of nonprofit messaging in a concise, well-written and impactful piece, you are well on your way to having a strong case for support.

Now that you have done the previous exercises, you may be able to convey your annual support campaign case statement more accurately and persuasively. The next exercises will help you to find the best answers to your individual case for giving and support.

Exercise

What are the top three messages that you want to convey with your annual support campaign case for giving?

1.
2.
3.

For each message, briefly explain who the target audience might be. Likely you will have multiple possible target audiences for each message.

CASE STATEMENT TARGET MESSAGE IDEA 1: POSSIBLE AUDIENCES

1a.
1b.
1c.
1d.

CASE STATEMENT TARGET MESSAGE IDEA 2: POSSIBLE AUDIENCES

2a.
2b.
2c.
2d.

(continued)

(*continued*)

CASE STATEMENT TARGET MESSAGE IDEA 3: POSSIBLE AUDIENCES

3a.
3b.
3c.
3d.

Now that we have listed some potential target audiences, are there additional messages some of the audiences might want to hear? How can you adjust your messaging now that you have considered the audience?

As you look at the possible audiences for your case statement messaging and at the messages themselves, you can begin to recognize possible stories from your work that might resonate with people.

What are the most heartfelt, convincing and insightful personal stories that you can tell about your nonprofit organization successes relating directly to the annual support campaign? Write possible story ideas here.

POSSIBLE CASE STATEMENT STORY IDEA 1

Possible Title _____
Who _____
What _____
Where _____
When _____
How _____

POSSIBLE CASE STATEMENT STORY IDEA 2

Possible Title _____
Who _____
What _____
Where _____
When _____
How _____

POSSIBLE CASE STATEMENT STORY IDEA 3

Possible Title _____

Who _____

What _____

Where _____

When _____

How _____

POSSIBLE CASE STATEMENT STORY IDEA 4

Possible Title _____

Who _____

What _____

Where _____

When _____

How _____

You can do this exercise multiple times and come up with several different stories of real impact that you can use to explain the important work that you are doing to your audiences. Hopefully, you can see how this type of exercise might help you to get to your end goal of creating a case for giving for your annual support campaign. Imagine if you did this exercise with others in your organization how many possible stories and messages you could come up with! This can be a powerful exercise for both staff and volunteers and can bring to the forefront stories and concepts that you may not have come up with otherwise.

Hint: If you cannot think of stories that are relevant to the ability of your program to make high-impact changes, you are probably just too far away from where the direct service work and transformational change occurs in your non-profit. Visit and talk directly to the people who are doing the front line work at your nonprofit. Likely you will hear, passionately and emphatically, the life-changing impact that your work is having.

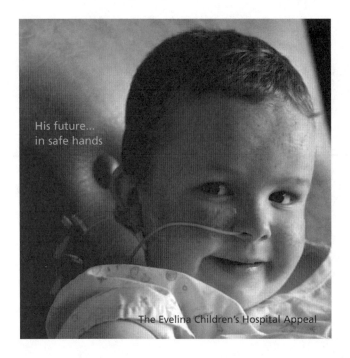

His future...
in safe hands

The Evelina Children's Hospital Appeal

At this point, it is important to be reminded that stories and other information are designed to educate and prompt donors without misleading them. Make sure to talk about your work and share stories that will motivate donors to understand the significant work that you do. Be certain that you do not alter the stories or mislead your donors in any way; doing so is a disservice to your organization and every other nonprofit in the world. Your stories are good enough without exaggeration. If they are not, focus on improving your program efforts before raising annual support campaign funds for it.

Another key point regarding annual support campaign case statements is to remember that, in this system of fundraising, volunteers play an integral role in our campaign's success or failure. We want to take every opportunity to involve and incorporate them in the tremendous work that we are doing. As we build the case for support, we should draw in and engage our volunteers in discussions about what is most important and how to fund it. These discussions not only build a stronger case statement and case for giving but they also build more committed volunteers who will help us with the work of fundraising when we start our campaign.

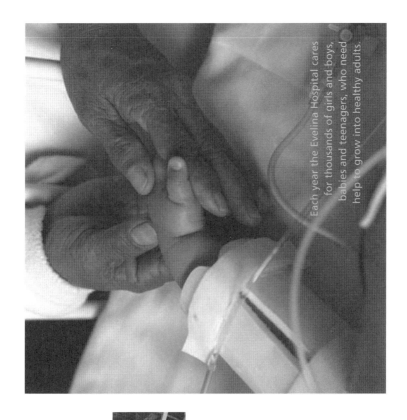

Each year the Evelina Hospital cares for thousands of girls and boys, babies and teenagers, who need help to grow into healthy adults.

Kyle's future

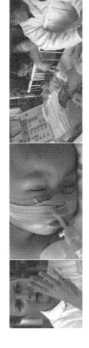

Kyle's **future couldn't be in safer hands.**

Fifteen months ago he was born with a serious lung condition which nearly ended his life. Now he's back in hospital with pneumonia. Without intensive care his lungs would collapse.

But with help from skilled staff and modern technology at the Evelina Children's Hospital, Kyle stands every chance of beating pneumonia and going from strength to strength.

Now, after years of careful planning, the Evelina is moving to a completely new purpose-built hospital at St Thomas'. The first new children's hospital in London for 100 years!

Opening in 2005, the new hospital is funded partly by the government, partly by Guy's and St Thomas' Charity, and partly by people who have generously supported the Evelina Children's Hospital Appeal.

With your help we can give many more children like Kyle the future their parents always dreamed of.

"We need to take advantage of the most advanced technology to give children the best possible care."

Toni Thomas, Senior Staff Nurse, Evelina Children's Hospital

Senior staff nurse, Toni Thomas, with baby Kyle, his mother and grandmother in the intensive care unit.

Our future

You've already helped us raise a magnificent £5 million towards the cost of equipping and furnishing the new Evelina Children's Hospital. But we still need your support to help us buy medical equipment, software, furnishings and toys.

Precision infusion pumps deliver exactly the right amount of antibiotics, drugs or other fluids into a child's veins. They also monitor the slightest changes to pressure in the child's arteries. The latest pumps are more precise and easier to use. They cost £2,200 each.

The latest type of life-support machine (here helping Holly) is far more flexible than older models. Instead of being simply on or off, the ventilators automatically adjust their support to match the child's own breath. Each one costs £30,000.

Parents like Holly's dad, Mark (above), can spend literally days sitting by their child's bed anxiously watching for signs of recovery. We want to buy 40 ergonomically designed chairs to make sure their wait is as comfortable as possible. They will cost £240 each.

A modern intensive care cot is highly specialised. The bed is completely height adjustable and the sides drop down quickly and easily so that doctors and nurses can reach a baby in an emergency. Parents can also get really close to comfort their baby with a cuddle. Each cot costs £2,000.

Please help us to make the new Evelina Hospital the best it can possibly be.

Doctors Rosenthal and Mookerjee operate to close a small hole in the heart of Quito, 11. Thanks to modern surgery Quito was well enough to go home the next day.

X-rays in the new Evelina Hospital will be stored on the latest digital system, making them easier to access and use.

Their futures

Ibrahim, 10, and his brother Musa, 14, both have sickle cell disease. Every month they travel from their home in Vauxhall to the Evelina for a 12 hour life-saving blood transfusion. "It's a lot to ask but they know they don't have a choice," says their father Abdul. Without the transfusions their blood will thicken and the boys will be vulnerable to strokes and severe, recurrent pain. Sickle cell disease is now the UK's most common genetic disorder.

Saoirse, 2, has already had two major heart operations – the first when she was only seven days old. Saoirse, from Folkestone, was born with the main arteries of her heart connected the wrong way round. Since birth she's been a frequent visitor to the Evelina. Her next operation will be to fit a pacemaker to regulate her heartbeat and stabilise her condition.

Holly, 8, was rushed to the Evelina from Brighton when she was diagnosed with pneumonia. Only the top third of her lungs was working. Each year the retrieval team brings over 600 children from all over the South East to the Evelina for emergency treatment. Children are stabilised at their local hospital, then brought to the Evelina for specialist care. Holly's pneumonia is responding well to treatment and she's expected to return home soon.

A new MRI scanner (being brought for the hospital by the Evelina Appeal) will scan blood vessels across the entire body. This will greatly assist with the diagnosis and treatment of Sickle Cell disease.

Ibrahim and Musa visit the Evelina for their blood transfusions to prevent the ill-effects of sickle cell disease.

Design by hrsgraphic.com Photography by Crispin Hughes Copy by Rodgers & Johns

Your help

Every pound we raise for the new Hospital can be used to buy specific items, because our fundraising costs are covered by Guy's and St. Thomas' Charity.

Your generosity has already enabled us to fund vital diagnostic, monitoring and anaesthetic equipment, parent beds and furniture for therapy and treatment rooms.

Of course we could manage with slightly less – with fewer advanced machines or slightly less child-friendly surroundings. But, frankly, we want children here to receive every advantage money can buy.

Thank you for your support.

Front cover: Oliver, 8, from Purley, pictured four days after his kidney transplant. Above: Harry Nyman, three weeks old, from North London, who will shortly be discharged following successful open heart surgery.

A big thank you to all the children and parents who allowed us to take their pictures and tell their stories in this leaflet.

The Evelina Children's Hospital Appeal, 1st Floor, West Wing, Counting House, Guy's Hospital, St Thomas Street, London SE1 9RT

Your help

A K I B A
academy of dallas

12324 Merit Drive
Dallas, TX 75251
www.akibaacademy.org

Now that you have done some of the hard work involved in building a strong case for giving to your annual support campaign, take some time to put your thoughts into a clear and concise document. This document should weave the most important of your earlier ideas into a coherent piece that conveys what it is you are trying to do and why you are trying to do it.

Once you have completed your own nonprofit annual campaign case for support, be sure to have many individuals read it and provide feedback. This can be an extremely valuable exercise with major donors or key volunteers in your nonprofit organization. By listening to what speaks to them, you can design a highly effective and motivating annual support campaign case statement.

HELP US BUILD OUR COMMUNITY.

The goal for the the Downtown Durham and Lakewood YMCAs is $150,000. Quite simply, without the support of people like you, we won't have the resources to continue to meet our growing area's vital needs.

Through the **WeBuildPeople** Campaign, we transform our community one child, one family, one relationship at a time. Your contribution makes it happen. Please add your support today.

Call 919-493-4502 to learn more.

webuildpeople.

www.ymcatriangle.org

Downtown Durham YMCA, 215 Morgan Street, Durham, NC 27701
Lakewood YMCA, 2119 Chapel Hill Road, Durham, NC 27707

117

$75 GAVE ME MY (FIRST SWIM) LESSONS. THANKS.

Skills development,
Character development,
Teamwork. Fun!

2004/2005
ANNUAL CAMPAIGN
DOWNTOWN
DURHAM/
LAKEWOOD
YMCA

webuildpeople.

118

There are many things to consider when you are reviewing your annual support campaign case for support. A case that contains more of the elements contained in the next checklist will likely be stronger and elicit greater and more positive response from your donors and prospects.

Checklist for Evaluating Your Annual Support Campaign Case for Support

- ❑ Does the piece focus on the reader rather than the organization?
- ❑ Does it talk about what the donor's money can do more than what the nonprofit organization can do?
- ❑ Is the typeface appropriate to your organization's appeal?
- ❑ Is the type large enough for easy reading by older people?
- ❑ Is there enough blank space to make it easy to read?
- ❑ Is the text readable, with short sentences and paragraphs?
- ❑ If you include graphs or charts, are they understandable and impactful?
- ❑ Is it educational while remaining focused on actually getting the gift?
- ❑ Is it short and to the point?
- ❑ Is it easy to understand?
- ❑ Does it emphasize "opportunity" for the donor rather than the "need" for your organization?
- ❑ If you use photographs, are they effective and cropped to maximize their impact? (Photos should rarely include more than two or three people; large group shots tend to lose their dramatic effect.)
- ❑ Does it evoke a sense of the history and long-term importance of your organization and the vital work that you are doing?
- ❑ Are the benefits to the donor clearly stated?
- ❑ Is the information presented in a logical order?
- ❑ Does it elicit emotional as well as statistical reasons to give?

❏ Does it tell your potential donors how their gift will make a difference?

❏ Is the paper itself attractive without looking expensive?

❏ Other?

Remember also to ask individuals outside of your organization to read your case for support and give you honest feedback before you go to press. It is easy to think that we are conveying something clearly when, in reality, we are using in-house terms, acronyms, or concepts that outsiders do not understand. By having people you trust but who are not too close to your organization analyze and provide feedback, you are helping to ensure that your case for support will be understandable and stirring to all who read it.

Summary

Having a well-thought-out case for support is a necessary part of any high functioning annual support campaign. This information conveys the essence of what your organization is doing and why it needs the support of its donors. The annual campaign case for support is explained in the written materials that you create and is used as the basis for asking your community for money.

There are many considerations when creating your case for annual campaign support. Asking key questions of your staff, volunteers and key constituencies offers insight as to what you should address in your annual support campaign. Questions such as, "Why do we need to raise the money?" and "Who are we raising the money to help?" assist your organization in framing the central issues in the campaign case. It also enables you to show how your nonprofit offers solutions and their associated costs. When you can tell people what you are going to do, what it will cost, and how their money can help you to change the world, you are well on your way to a strong annual support campaign.

The best annual campaign case addresses issues of both the heart and the mind. A well conceived case for support shows everyone involved in your campaign from the staff member to the volunteer to the donor why you need to raise the money, why they should be involved, and why they need to support your cause.

## CHAPTER 5

Recruiting Volunteers

After reading this chapter, you will be able to:

- Acknowledge the reasons why you should and need to recruit campaign volunteers.
- Determine who in your community would make the best volunteers and why.
- Understand how to recruit volunteers for your annual support campaign.
- Establish the roles that volunteers play in a high-functioning annual support campaign.

An adage about the high-functioning annual support campaign says, "It is two campaigns. The first campaign is for volunteers and the second campaign is for dollars." If you do not focus your time and energy on the first campaign of getting volunteers, then your second campaign for dollars will never be as successful as it could be.

How do we get our constituency engaged in the annual support campaign? The short answer is that you build relationships and you ask. The longer answer is this chapter.

Understanding Your Constituency

Who in your programs loves you? This question can help you identify and begin to select who in your programs might be an advocate for you in your annual support campaign.

If you think about the individuals who are excited about what you do, you will already have a great idea about who might be willing to volunteer for you. Think about the people who participate now in the great work that you do. Think about which individuals are the most helpful. Think about who takes the most advantage of the super work that you are already doing in the community.

Exercise

Write down the names of 10 (or more) of the most passionate people you know who are involved with the work that you do. It does not matter how they are related to your organization. These individuals could be community members, members of your constituency, or others. Only list people who already volunteer in some way for your organization.

1.
2.
3.
4.
5.
6.
7.
8.
9.
10.

Have each person on your staff and volunteer team make a list of individuals who are enthusiastic about the work that you do. If you cannot write down 10 names, that may indicate that you are too far away from the impactful work that you are doing or that you are just doing a poor job of promoting volunteerism in general. Sometimes this happens in administrative positions; it indicates that you may need to get closer to the mission work your organization is doing. It may also be a sign that your nonprofit organization needs to branch out more in building relationships.

What if everyone close to your organization performed the same exercise? Imagine how many names of enthusiastic individuals could be identified. The more you do this exercise at the staff and volunteer level of your organization, the more likely you are to grow your volunteer workforce to its greatest size and power.

Notice that, in the exercise, we did not ask "Who would make a great fundraising volunteer?" By looking for people with passion, we are looking first for people who believe in the tremendous work that we are doing. We are not looking for people whom we think of as fundraisers; we are looking for people we believe have passion for the work we are doing. That enthusiasm is a good first indicator of someone who might be willing and able to tell the story of our organization in the community. That passion is what can help us to communicate the significant work that we are doing. That passion can carry volunteers through a tough dialogue with a potential donor and is conveyed through their words, ideas, and body language. The energy that a person has for your work and your organization can overcome obstacles and help an individual shine as an advocate. It is one of my favorite criteria for great fundraising volunteers.

Although passion can be grown within individuals, it can be found clearly within those people who believe strongly in the work that we do at our nonprofit organizations each and every day. Why not harness that power? We can and should—but first we have to recognize the passion and then ask people to help.

Before Volunteers Get Involved

People want to know certain things before they agree to get involved in our work. A few things that they will likely want to know include:

- How much time is involved?
- What do you want me to do?

- What does success look like?

- Who will work with me on this project?

- What tools will I get to help me with this project?

- Is the organization really behind this?

- Will my time be valued and well used?

- Will I be trained on what it is I am supposed to do?

- If I have questions, whom can I go to for help?

- Other?!

Individuals will have many questions before or after they accept a volunteer assignment. If you want people to commit to your nonprofit, you must be ready to address their concerns and questions. But even before this occurs, you should have something more, if at all possible: a relationship.

Building Relationships

Relationship is a scary word for some of us in fundraising because of the time commitment needed or the history that may be lacking between the fundraiser and the potential donor. However, if you are to be successful in your nonprofit work, you must be willing to form and grow relationships with others who are involved in the work that you do—both staff members and volunteers alike. Some of us are able to go through our day sitting behind a computer or a desk, having limited, easy relationships with our closest work colleagues. In today's competitive nonprofit world, however, we must be willing to form relationships with individuals who exude passion and discover those who have as-yet untapped excitement about the work that we do. In order to do this, we must reach out so that we can connect with people. People sometimes will reach out to us, but if you are to be most successful, you cannot count on this. If you want to connect with people, you are well served to make the first move. Your best decision is to reach out, take time with someone, make a new friend, or grow an old one. Deep relationships will do more to help your cause and ultimately your fundraising efforts. While they take time, they pay priceless returns in a variety of ways, including fundraising.

So much of financial development and ultimately fundraising work goes back to the relationships that we have with people. I have worked with many nonprofits where employees believe that their job is to provide a service or program to the community that they serve. They believe that their only role is to go to work and perform a specific job, such as keeping children safe or teaching students or protecting a special population of people or animals or land.

These employees are wrong.

The job of each of us in the nonprofit sector is certainly to perform many of these functions, but everyone must be aware of the need to build relationships with people who can help us do even more of the work that we are doing. Our nonprofits are only as good as they truly can be when we involve and engage our communities in making their missions happen. If we do not take the time and effort to involve others in the work that we do, we are limiting our ability to fully utilize our community resources to the betterment of our organizational mission. We are limiting our ability to spread our message and educate our constituency. We are limiting our ability to meet our societal objectives. And, last but not least, we are limiting our ability to raise charitable funds. No matter if you are the largest university or the largest human services agency or the largest environmental organization in the world; if you are not engaging others in the critical work that you are doing, your organization is destined to be an underachiever.

By engaging others in the work that we do, we can all be exponentially stronger.

If we were to analyze the most effective nonprofits in the world, I believe that you would see that they have tapped into their community, however large, and meaningfully involved them in some way. If each of us does not take advantage of the relationships that we can have and develop, we will never be as strong as we can be. And we will never raise as much money in our annual support campaigns as we could.

Reasons People Will Want to Volunteer for Your Nonprofit

Your Mission

People believe strongly in the work that you are doing in the community that you are serving. They want to be a part of something bigger than themselves; they want to help improve the issues that your nonprofit is addressing. People want to be involved in work with true impact, and your organization can be the one to provide this outlet for them. Ask people to do something really meaningful with your organization and you will be pleasantly surprised by the results.

Chance to Own Something

Most people are looking for their lives to have real value, and they find it in different ways. For some, part of the meaning is making a difference in the world around them. You can be the organization to show them how they can make a difference, through their work on your annual support campaign. Imagine how it would feel to know that *you* were the direct cause of making a specific positive event occur. You can give that reward to people who volunteer for your annual support campaign. By involving them as fundraising volunteers, you can show them the direct results of the money that they raised. Without those funds, good things will not happen. They get to own that valuable experience and feeling in exchange for their help on the campaign.

Opportunity to Practice and Grow Leadership Experience

Some for-profit companies actually make it a point to send their employees out into the nonprofit world to gain experience and practice with leadership. Many corporate executives have recognized that the nonprofit organizations in their community are a fertile training ground for their own executives. They know that there are few places better to learn how to do a lot with a little than the nonprofit sector. These companies recognize that their employees can learn everything from leadership development to public speaking and many things in between. By recognizing that you provide a unique opportunity for people who want to grow and develop in these ways, you begin to understand that volunteering in the annual support campaign can be a transformational experience both personally and professionally for those who choose to be involved.

They Get to Be More Deeply Involved

Volunteers in your annual support campaign will become some of your closest organizational friends. They will know your nonprofit organization better; they will know your staff better; they will know your mission better; they will understand the population that you serve better and they will understand the true value of your work better. Engaged volunteers will come to know you in ways that others just do not have the ability to see or understand. This experience can make them your strongest advocates, donors, and volunteer leaders. This experience can also pay huge dividends for your organization over time, in terms of securing, identifying, and cultivating both committed volunteers and major donors.

Volunteers Gain Networking Opportunities

In a high-functioning annual support campaign, volunteers meet new people, connect with them, and make friends. In life, people often want to meet others and have the opportunity to get to know them. They might share common interests related to work or personal life, or they may be interacting with someone who opens their eyes to a whole new experience. The annual support campaign gives individuals this chance. I have seen many lifelong friendships come out of people working side by side on annual support campaigns and it can be one of the most valuable aspects for some people of the overall annual campaign experience. By giving people the opportunity to meet and get to know others, you are giving people a great gift that they might not be able to achieve in other aspects of their daily life.

People Like to Be on a Winning Team

Working on a successful annual support campaign can be invigorating and uplifting for people who are involved with making it happen. Giving your volunteers the chance to be engaged with a project that is actually changing the world for the better can provide them with strong and life-changing experiences. Think about a time when you were part of something bigger than yourself and it went well. You probably felt proud, empowered, energized, and many other really positive emotions. The fact that you remember it is proof itself. Your volunteers will feel the same way when they are part of your triumphant annual support campaign team.

The annual support campaign can be a beneficial connecting experience for your volunteers and staff. Volunteers will more fully embrace your organization and your mission if they can be more intrinsically involved in actually helping to make your work happen. Annual support campaign volunteers will become some of your organization's greatest volunteers. Be sure to treat them like the treasure they really are.

It Just Feels Good to Help Others

People really do like to help and feel needed. Some people are involved in civic activities throughout their lives. It is a part of who they are in the world. For others, volunteering is a new and different experience. These people may never have been a part of something so large or inspiring before. The reasons for wanting to help, and the benefits received, are as unique and varied as the individuals. But what is true for all volunteers is when an annual support campaign is run well, volunteers feel appreciated and valued. They have helped others through their work and can truly quantify the difference they have made through their efforts. Annual support campaign volunteers know that they have made the world a better place. And that feels really good.

Now that we have looked a bit at what volunteers get out of the experience, it is good to be reminded of a few key ingredients that these same volunteers bring to your organization.

Volunteers Become Some of Your Greatest Philanthropists

One of the things that annual support campaign volunteers do is make their own gift to the campaign. Seasoned and well-trained volunteers give their gift knowing that when they go and ask others to give, they may be asked how much they gave and why. When someone gives repeatedly to your campaign, over time, their interest, engagement, and commitment to your organization almost always grows. I have seen countless cases of annual support campaign volunteers who start out in their first year making a small gift, then by year 3 or 4 are making much larger annual gifts. Since, over time, they are telling the story of your organization to others and because they are out in the community themselves, representing you to others, they become a very real and active part of your nonprofit team and workforce. Their involvement intrinsically deepens through the process, and thus, these volunteers become your biggest advocates. This almost inevitably makes their commitment—including the dollar kind—go up.

Giving Is Part of Their Job Description

As described in the last section, one part of the job description of an annual support campaign volunteer is to make a gift to the annual support campaign before asking others to do so. While this may seem like a simple thing, you must not leave it to chance. You need to state it clearly from the beginning, that volunteers who will be asking others for financial donations, must make their own contribution first. When it is in the job description of volunteers to give their gifts first, before they ask others to do so, you will get lots of donations before you even begin the campaign. In the most successful annual support campaigns that I have worked with over the years, it is absolutely not by coincidence that the most outstanding volunteers were also the most significant donors. They are, often times, the same people.

By this point, I hope I have made the case that volunteers can be worth their weight in gold (literally!) to your nonprofit organization. With such powerful advocates and team members on our fundraising annual support campaign teams, our nonprofit organizations can accomplish more than ever. We know what strong volunteers can do for us, but what do they look like?

There are many people that we could ask to be involved in our organizations, our programs, and our annual support campaigns. These people come in all shapes and sizes, but we can identify many characteristics of vibrant fundraising volunteers. The next section serves as a solid beginning to pinpoint and ultimately recruit high-functioning volunteers for your annual support campaign.

What Do Strong Fundraisers Look Like?

Organizational Leaders

An obvious place to look for annual support volunteers is in the leadership already established in your organization. Consider board members, committee members, task force managers, group leaders of all dimensions, or just the quiet leader who helps you to make things happen in your nonprofit. All of these

---

Exercise

Write the names of individuals that fit the profile just described. They are likely great candidates to become volunteers in your annual support campaign.

1.
2.
3.
4.
5.
6.

---

individuals should be considered as primary prospects to become potential fundraising volunteers in your annual support campaign.

Community Leaders

You and others likely perceive certain people in your community as the ones to follow. These leaders make positive changes occur on a daily, weekly, or yearly basis. Although they may not always be the first to speak, they are almost always listened to on key community issues or challenges. When people in such positions become involved in your annual support campaign, they can bring with them great change and many other individuals. These people usually have not acquired such high profiles by lazing around, so they are often busy with business efforts and perhaps other community projects. While they may or may not say yes when you first ask them to become an annual support campaign volunteer, if you can get them involved, you can make tremendous things happen in your campaign in both the short and long term.

Exercise

Write the names of individuals who fit the profile just described. They are likely great candidates to become volunteers in your annual support campaign.

1.
2.
3.
4.
5.
6.

Passionate

People who are passionate about the work that you do are another obvious place to look for annual support campaign volunteers. Individuals who know what you do and are excited and motivated by your efforts, are often able and motivated to help you. These enthusiastic and zealous people can make especially persuasive and diligent volunteers in your annual campaign effort.

Exercise

Write the names of individuals who fit the profile just described. They are likely great candidates to become volunteers in your annual support campaign.

1.
2.
3.
4.
5.
6.

Well Organized

Busy and well organized people make time to do the things that are important to them. By utilizing individuals who are good time managers and well organized, you bring into your efforts those who can help to make

---

Exercise

Write the names of individuals who fit the profile just described. They are likely great candidates to become volunteers in your annual support campaign.

1.
2.
3.
4.
5.
6.

---

the campaign run more smoothly as well as complete it in a timely manner. Those people with honed or natural organizational skills, from the big picture to the seemingly small details, bring a talent that is often overlooked until you are in the middle of the campaign. Often times, these people just get things done.

Compassionate

There are those among us who try to make positive change by saving the world one unit at a time, one person, one polar bear, one puppy at a time. These individuals are compelled by the understanding that one person can make a difference . . . one at a time. As Mother Teresa said, "I can love the person in front of me." Compassionate people can carry out their actions through your annual support campaign to change the situation, one entity at a time. Likely there is little better way to change the world that is your community than by doing it one step at a time through your annual support campaign.

Exercise

Write the names of individuals who fit the profile just described. They are likely great candidates to become volunteers in your annual support campaign.

1.
2.
3.
4.
5.
6.

Visionaries

Individuals who have great vision for the future often can see the power and benefit of the annual support campaign. Having a strong annual campaign helps to make sure that your nonprofit organization can survive in both good times and bad. It helps to stabilize your annual revenue streams in ways that other programming cannot do. It makes your nonprofit more self reliant by making it more responsible for its own destiny by owning annual fundraising. Visionaries understand the changing dynamics of the nonprofit sector and often will recognize the value of building long-term sustainable programming that is accompanied by a high potential benefit to the organization.

Exercise

Write the names of individuals who fit the profile just described. They are likely great candidates to become volunteers in your annual support campaign.

1.
2.
3.
4.
5.
6.

IN THE REAL WORLD

At a nonprofit I worked with, as part of a large federated nonprofit earlier In my career, a group of visionary leaders came together to discuss doing the first annual support campaign. They decided to follow the lead of similar organizations to undertake the organization's first such campaign. They believed that a strong annual campaign was the best way to financially stabilize their organization in the short and long term. They also believed that it would help to more fully explain the work that they were doing in the community as a whole. The first year, not only did they surpass the monetary goal they set for themselves, but they also set the course to continue the annual campaign on a yearly basis. Every year since that first campaign many years ago, they have set an even higher goal, which they have ultimately surpassed through the dedicated work of many staff members and volunteers. Tens of millions of dollars have been raised that would not have been raised otherwise. Also, many relationships have been built that have resulted in large capital and endowment gifts. The annual support campaign was a direct result of visionary people becoming engaged and committing to making a long-term, sustainable positive change for the organization. It has paid tremendous dividends and continues to do so to this day.

Well Spoken

Some people are eloquent and charismatic when speaking to groups. They are calm, descriptive, and persuasive in their message. These individuals who present themselves and their ideas well, are often good candidates for recruitment to the annual support campaign. They can articulate ideas and concepts clearly so that others can, and are interested in embracing them. Volunteers who are well spoken can share the nuances of where support goes as well as why each of us should support the annual support campaign. They also can serve in various leadership roles in the campaign structure, as appropriate.

Exercise

Write the names of individuals who fit the profile just described. They are likely great candidates to become volunteers in your annual support campaign.

1.
2.
3.
4.
5.
6.

Goal Oriented

People who are goal oriented can make strong annual support campaign volunteers because they embrace a goal and objective for themselves and others, then hold themselves accountable for making it happen. Goal oriented people take on responsibilities and objectives and then work tirelessly to make them happen. This characteristic can be extremely powerful as they go out into the community to tell the story of your organization in order to raise charitable funds. If you can harness the energy of goal-oriented people within your organization toward the annual support campaign, they can and often do bring great strength to their work.

Exercise

Write the names of individuals who fit the profile just described. They are likely great candidates to become volunteers in your annual support campaign.

1.
2.
3.
4.
5.
6.

Influential

Certain people in your midst can make things happen because of the influence that they carry due to their professional position, their social status, or their

---

Exercise

Write the names of individuals who fit the profile just described. They are likely great candidates to become volunteers in your annual support campaign.

1.
2.
3.
4.
5.
6.

---

place in your organization. Like the leader, these individuals can help make positive change in your organization and can help to determine the direction or path of your annual support campaign. With the ability to persuade and win over others, they can encourage involvement on many levels. Overall, these individuals have the ability to create measurable change in your annual support campaign.

Networkers

Some people in your organization bring with them the gift of gab. They know who is who at your nonprofit as well as in the community. These people seem to know everyone, and everyone seems to know them. Over the years, I have watched a number of colleagues who, naturally, fluidly, got to know seemingly everyone in the community. The beauty was that they did it genuinely, as a part of their inherent style, and it was an unbelievable bonus to our organization. If you can bring networkers into your volunteer efforts, they will likely communicate with and contact many others with relative ease because they already have established relationships and influence with so many people. These people are yet another powerful source of energy and volunteerism to your annual support campaign.

Exercise

Write the names of individuals who fit the profile just described. They are likely great candidates to become volunteers in your annual support campaign.

1.
2.
3.
4.
5.
6.

Finishers

These people get things done and have the ability to follow up and follow through on making things happen. Often they make the repeated attempts at tasks and do not let up on that last 10%. The small details matter to these folks. If you can get them involved, you stand a great chance of them doing what they say they will in the time allotted. They are great people to have on the team if you can gain their commitment.

Exercise

Write the names of individuals who fit the profile just described. They are likely great candidates to become volunteers in your annual support campaign.

1.
2.
3.
4.
5.
6.

Cheerleaders

Most people can recognize these people easily. They have a tremendously positive attitude that they eagerly share with others. They bring an upbeat spirit and optimism to your annual support campaign and are enjoyable and fun to be around. When the going gets tough, it can be great to have some cheerleader-type volunteers in your midst. They can be great catalysts to people who are timid, reluctant, or retiring. Their can-do spirit will do much to breed continued success and enthusiasm in your annual support campaign in good times and in bad.

Exercise

Write the names of individuals who fit the profile just described. They are likely great candidates to become volunteers in your annual support campaign.

1.
2.
3.
4.
5.
6.

Recipients

Depending on the situation at our nonprofit organizations, there are times when we can engage and involve those who benefit from our annual support work in the actual effort of raising the money. Because these individuals know firsthand where the money goes, they can be strong advocates for the value and treasure of the money raised. A great example of this is college students who receive scholarships and who also give their time as an annual support campaign

---

Exercise

Write the names of individuals who fit the profile just described. They are likely great candidates to become volunteers in your annual support campaign.

1.
2.
3.
4.
5.
6.

---

volunteer. The ability to explain the value of a contribution from a firsthand perspective makes these volunteers a convincing part of the testimony of the annual support campaign.

Community Activists

Some individuals and groups in your community are involved in charitable work on a wide-scale basis. They are used to the work of fundraising and always seem to be involved in the important work of helping charitable organizations raise funds to further their missions. These community activists are often well connected and highly capable in the art and skill of fundraising. The increased community credibility and volunteer expertise they bring can greatly help your annual support campaign.

Exercise

Write the names of individuals who fit the profile just described. They are likely great candidates to become volunteers in your annual support campaign.

1.
2.
3.
4.
5.
6.

Senior Managers

These people are in a position to gather many others around an issue. Senior managers begin their volunteer involvement process with the advantage of almost always having supervisory and other influence over large groups of people. When a corporation, for example, takes on a community initiative, it can become a cause that many of their employees rally around. Due to their supervisory position and sphere of influence, senior managers can mobilize their teams with relative ease. These people do not have to only be in the corporate world; whatever sector they are in, the senior manager type can quickly mobilize and garner the attention of many individuals.

Exercise

Write the names of individuals who fit the profile just described. They are likely great candidates to become volunteers in your annual support campaign.

1.
2.
3.
4.
5.
6.

Well Resourced

These people have a large amount of financial resources at their disposal. Because they can make large gifts, they can help your organization reach its annual support goal more easily. Since these people have financial security and the

---

Exercise

Write the names of individuals who fit the profile just described. They are likely great candidates to become volunteers in your annual support campaign.

1.
2.
3.
4.
5.
6.

---

potential to make large philanthropic gifts, they can more easily agree to and attempt large annual support campaign goals and objectives.

Programmatically Connected

Think of volunteers who are already involved in your programs or projects. These are the individuals who read to children, help with administrative work, or prepare and serve meals to the hungry. Because these individuals are already giving their time, working in the annual support campaign can be a logical extension of their active commitment to your organization. Additionally, they are often well versed in your organizational mission so they bring this expertise and experience to your annual campaign.

Exercise

Write the names of individuals who fit the profile just described. They are likely great candidates to become volunteers in your annual support campaign.

1.
2.
3.
4.
5.
6.

Retired

Possibly the most underutilized group of our society is the retired sector. Often they have enough time available to be very involved and can spend the necessary hours accomplishing many components of your campaign. Retired citizens often are looking for places to get involved, feel needed, use their skills, stay connected, and remain vital. They may have the time to do many time-consuming administrative tasks as well as giving the extra effort to build relationships or help plan events. They may even come to the table with many long-standing relationships in the community.

Others in your community who are not retired also may have this time and flexibility. The person who works from home might enjoy the networking, or the stay-at-home parent might be thrilled to have some flexible involvement with the community.

Exercise

Write the names of individuals who fit the profile just described. They are likely great candidates to become volunteers in your annual support campaign.

1.
2.
3.
4.
5.
6.

Perhaps you can think of more types of supporters who can help in your annual support campaign. As you think about and identify people who can make community change, you will identify patterns of personality and behavior. There may be other groups in your midst not covered here that you can consider analyzing for possible volunteer recruitment.

TIPS AND TECHNIQUES

Once a month or so, at staff, board, and committee meetings, bring out a flip chart page with "New Potential Volunteers" listed on it. Encourage staff members to add names to the list as they get to know people associated with the organization or around the community. This exercise can be brief, but it does five things:

(continued)

Continued

1 It keeps track of potential volunteers throughout the year.

2 Seeing the list each month keeps these volunteers on staff members' minds so they can continue to build relationships.

3 It encourages your staff to think of new people they have encountered as potential volunteers.

4 It reduces the need for the big brainstorming session, and the risk of forgetting someone that is not as "high profile," when it comes time for the annual support campaign.

5 It shows staff members how sincere this effort is and how they can be a big part of it.

Make it fun! Have a prize for the person who names the most potential volunteers over the months.

A time saver: Keeping this list of potential volunteers and the staff or volunteer who suggested them, will give you a resource to use when determining who might be a good person to go on the volunteer recruitment call.

Let us now look at how to get these people connected to your nonprofit and how an actual annual support campaign recruitment call might go.

Performing Volunteer Recruitment

Information to Make the Volunteer Recruitment Ask

Before you make a volunteer recruitment call, there are a few things that you can do to get ready. Obviously, the more established your relationship is with the prospect, the easier the call will be to make. It is for this reason that relationship building (discussed more fully in Chapter 7) is one important aspect of nonprofit management and operations.

Assuming you have some relationship with the prospect, these five materials will help you as you progress:

1. Volunteer contact information card

2. Volunteer job descriptions for possible recruitment positions

3. Annual support campaign pledge card. This is the card that is filled out by the volunteer with the prospective donor to keep track of pledges made toward the campaign.

4. A case statement for this year's campaign. If you do not yet have this information created in brochure form, on a website or some other place (which you should!), pull together the best information you have to make the call. Ideally, the case statement outlines how the money will be spent. Depending on the stage of the campaign, you may not have created this document yet.

5. An annual support campaign calendar.

If you do not have an established relationship with the volunteer prospect whom you are about to call on, you can use the meeting as an opportunity to create and build that relationship. While it is always better to build upon an existing relationship than it is to start a new one on a volunteer recruitment call, go forth with a positive attitude, and consider this an opportunity to do both in one call. Be sure to keep building on this new relationship in the future!

Getting Ready to Make the Volunteer Recruitment Ask

It is just as important that you are ready to make the call as it is that you have your information ready. There are three key things that you can do as you ready yourself to make your first phone call or personal visit.

1. Think about why the mission is important and why you are involved or inspired to be involved with this campaign.

2. Learn what you can about your prospects' involvement with your non-profit organization as well as their other interests.

3. Decide how much to ask your prospects for as a gift when you recruit them as volunteers. Because you are already contacting them, this is a great time to make the ask for the annual support campaign. By doing this, you

are also accomplishing one of the first line items in their job description if they decide to become volunteers.

Deciding how much to ask a prospect to give, which is addressed in more depth in Chapter 7, is sometimes more art than science. There may be data, such as previous giving levels or other giving capacity information, but often with annual campaign work, little is known about how much prospects truly can give or afford. Many times, a "best guess" is made and an ask is attempted. While this method is less than optimal, it is important to understand that often you should do the best that you can with the information that you have. Formal prospect research may or may not be available, and part of the annual support campaign is learning about your prospects. Just think, when you track this data well this year, it will be ready and available for you to use in next year's campaign! More about this important topic will be discussed in Chapter 7.

Things to Bring on a Volunteer Recruitment Call

- A chart of the campaign volunteer structure (see Chapter 6).

- Campaign calendar showing what is happening when in your campaign schedule (Exhibit 5.1).

- Recruitment meeting outline to keep your meeting on track. Think of this as a beginning script for your recruiting call (see page 154).

- Appropriate job descriptions for possible recruiting positions (Exhibit 5.2).

- Document of additional, potential volunteer prospects. It is part of the position description of the volunteer you are speaking with, to help recruit these additional volunteers (Exhibit 5.3).

- Volunteer Recruitment Information Card asking for key personal communication information (e-mail, phone, mailing address, spouse's name, favorite nonprofit organization program, etc.) (Exhibit 5.4).

- Pledge card to get their gift (Exhibit 5.5).

EXHIBIT 5.1

Example of Campaign Calendar for Chair

201_ Annual Campaign Calendar
Making a Difference for Our Community

Thursday, June 18	-	**Division Chair's Luncheon – Noon**
Thursday, August 6	-	**Team Leader's Organizational Meeting—Noon**
Tuesday, September 29	-	**Coaching Session/Training for all Volunteers – 7:00 PM**
Thursday, October 1	-	**MAKE UP Coaching Session/Training for those not able to attend September 22 – 7:00 AM**
Thursday, October 8	-	**Kickoff for All Volunteers – 7:00 PM**
Thursday, October 15	-	**Call-In or Drop Off Report Night—5:00—7:30**
Thursday, October 22	-	**Division Chairs Team Meetings**
Thursday, October 29	-	**In-Person Report Meeting for All Volunteers – 7:00 PM**
Thursday, November 5	-	**Call-In or Drop Off Report Night—5:00—7:30**
Thursday, November 12	-	**Campaign Victory Celebration – 7:00 PM**

XYZ
Changing Lives
For the Better

- Reminders and tips for asking. (see pages 214–215).

- "10 steps to Making a Successful Annual Support Campaign Ask" (see pages 217–219).

- Blank note card and stamped envelope addressed to whom you are meeting

Getting the Personal Meeting

Contacting someone by telephone or other electronic means is a great way to gain an even more personal contact. Depending on you, the prospect, and your relationship with him or her, electronic means such as e-mail or text message may even make sense. The goal with any communication should be that it is as personal and as relationship building as possible. As a new demographic

EXHIBIT 5.2

Job Descriptions for Volunteer Campaign Chairs

XYZ Nonprofit Organization
201_ Annual Support Campaign Chair's Job Description

1. Serve in a key leadership role as the Annual Campaign Chair of the XYZ Nonprofit Organization's 201_ "Annual Giving" Campaign.

2. Identify and Recruit (on a face-to-face basis) four Division Chairs (Major Gifts Chair, Community Gifts Chair, Board Solicitation Chair and Staff Campaign Chair) to serve in your campaign organization by June 4, 201_.

3. Make sure that your Division Chairs attend a Division Chair's Organizational meeting on June 18, 201_ and that you attend with them. The campaign plan and calendar will be shared at this time.

4. Help assure that your Division Chairs complete the recruitment of their Team Leaders by July 17, 201_.

5. Attend a Team Leader's Organizational meeting (with those selected by our Division Leaders) on August 6, 201_.

6. Attend one Campaigner Training meeting during the week of September 29, 201_.

7. Chair the Campaign Kick-Off Dinner on October 8, 201_.

8. Make your own generous contribution to the Campaign prior to the Kick-Off.

9. Select, Call (face-to-face), "Tell the XYZ Nonprofit Story," and secure a gift from six donor prospects over the six-week money campaign period. (Ask the Four Chairs you help recruit plus at least two more individuals.)

10. Stay in touch with your Division Chairs regarding their division's progress throughout the campaign. Urge attendance as appropriate at campaign report meetings during the public phase.

11. Reside as chair at the Victory Celebration Dinner on November 12, 201_.

XYZ Nonprofit Organization
201_ Annual Support Campaign Division Chair's Job Description

1. Serve in a key leadership role as a Division Chair in the XYZ Nonprofit Organization's "Annual Giving" Campaign.

(continued)

2. Attend a Division Chair's Organizational Meeting with the Annual Campaign Chair on June 18, 201_.
3. Identify and Recruit (preferably on a face-to-face basis) four Team Leaders to serve in your division with you by July 17, 201_.
4. Assure the attendance of your Team Leaders at the Team Leader's Organizational Meeting on August 6, 201_.
5. Attend the Team Leader's Organizational Meeting with your Team Leaders on August 6, 201_.
6. Assure that your Team Leaders complete the recruitment of their team's Campaigners by September 15, 201_.
7. Attend one Campaigner Training Session during the week of September 29, 201_.
8. Attend the Campaign Kickoff Dinner on October 8, 201_.
9. Make your own generous contribution to Campaign prior to the Kickoff.
10. Select, Call On (face-to-face), ''Tell the XYZ Nonprofit Story,'' and Secure a financial gift from at least six donor prospects over the six-week campaign period. (Your four team members plus at least two more.)
11. Encourage your Team Leaders to ensure that team results are accurately reported at weekly report meetings.
12. Attend the Victory Celebration Dinner on November 12, 201_.

XYZ Nonprofit Organization 201_ Annual Support Campaign Team Leader's Job Description

1. Serve in a key leadership role as a Team Leader in the XYZ Nonprofit Organization's 201_ Annual Support Campaign.
2. Attend a Team Leader's Organizational Meeting with your Division Chairs on August 6, 201_.
3. Identify and Recruit (preferably face-to-face) four Team Campaigners to serve on your team with you by September 15, 201_.
4. Assure the attendance of your campaigners at the Campaigners Training Session during the week of September 29, 201_. This session will prepare you and your Team Campaigners to ''Tell the XYZ Nonprofit

(continued)

EXHIBIT 5.2

Job Descriptions for Volunteer Campaign Chairs (Continued)

Story'' and encourage others to make a financial gift to XYZ Nonprofit Organization. The sessions offered are:

Tuesday	September 29	7–8 PM	at XYZ
Thursday	October 1	7–8 AM	at XYZ

5. Attend the Campaign Kickoff Dinner on October 8, 201_.

6. Make your own generous contribution to the Campaign prior to the Kickoff.

7. Select, call on (face-to-face), ''Tell the XYZ Nonprofit Organization Story,'' and secure a financial gift from six donor prospects over the four-week campaign period.

8. Encourage your Team Campaigners to make their four (at least) donor prospect calls on a timely basis and report their results at weekly report meetings.

9. Report your results at the report meetings.

Thursday	October 15	5:00—7:30 PM	at the XYZ
Thursday	October 22	Team Meeting	TBA
Thursday	October 29	7:00 PM	at the XYZ
Thursdays	November 5	5:00 – 7:30 PM	at the XYZ

10. Attend the Victory Celebration Dinner on Thursday, November 12, 201_.

XYZ Nonprofit Organization
201_ Annual Support Campaign Campaigner's
Job Description

1. Serve in a key role as a Campaigner in the XYZ Nonprofit Organization's 201_ Annual Support Campaign.

2. Attend a one-time Campaigners Training Session during the week of September 29, 201_. This session will prepare you to ''Tell the XYZ Story'' and encourage others to make a financial gift to XYZ. The sessions offered are:

(continued)

| Tuesday | September 29 | 7–8 PM | at XYZ |
| Thursday | October 1 | 7–8 AM | at XYZ |

3. Attend the Campaign Kickoff Dinner on October 8, 201_. (Time and location to be announced.)

4. Make your own generous contribution to the Campaign prior to the Kickoff.

5. Select, call on a (face-to-face), "Tell the XYZ Story," and secure a financial gift from six donor prospects over the four-week campaign period.

6. Report your results at the report meetings.

Thursday	October 15	5:00—7:30 PM	at the XYZ
Thursday	October 22	Team Meeting	TBA
Thursday	October 29	7:00 PM	at the XYZ
Thursday	November 5	5:00 – 7:30 PM	at the XYZ

7. Attend the Victory Celebration Dinner on November 12, 201_.

EXHIBIT 5.3

List of Possible Volunteer Prospects

Richard Foot	Committee Member, Donor
Judy Bright	Board Trustee
Mike Bussey	Donor, Board Member
Robert Clark	Active Community Member
Daniel Harris	Committee Member, Major Donor
Michael Harrison	Committee Member, Donor
Vanessa Boulous	Former Chair, Committee Member, Donor
Chuck Ainsworth	Committee Member, Donor

EXHIBIT 5.4

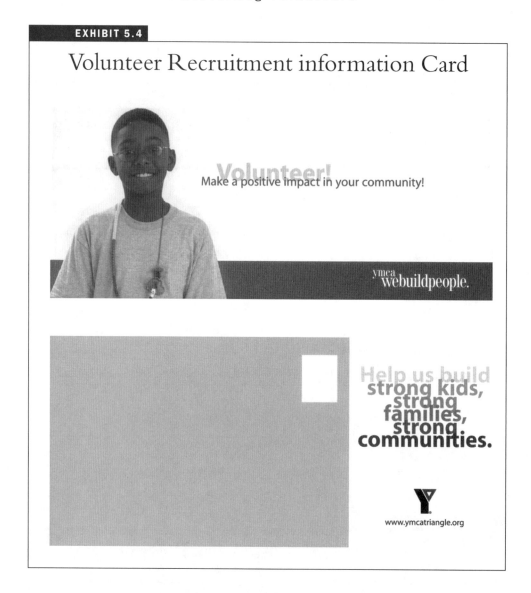

Volunteer Recruitment information Card

Volunteer!
Make a positive impact in your community!

ymca
webuildpeople.

Help us build
strong kids,
strong
families,
strong
communities.

Y

www.ymcatriangle.org

develops in our society, this may mean different things to different donor and prospect populations. Often times, younger people use many more of the technological possibilities available and find them both natural and productive in gaining access to prospects. The goal is to get the person to give you a truly and fully committed yes. Experience has shown me time and time again that keeping contact as personal as possible is still the best way. For me, this has been using the telephone and then making a personal visit, but your situation may be

EXHIBIT 5.5

Pledge Card Example

Y ymca **webuildpeople.**

Desiring to help others through YMCA financial assistance, I pledge the following amount to the branch(es) checked:

☐ A.E. Finley YMCA $ _____
☐ Camps Sea Gull/Seafarer $ _____
☐ Cary Family YMCA $ _____
☐ Central YMCA $ _____
☐ Johnston County YMCA $ _____
☐ Kerr Family YMCA $ _____
☐ Lee County YMCA $ _____

☐ Southwest Wake YMCA $ _____
☐ YMCA of Garner $ _____
☐ Big Brothers Big Sisters $ _____
☐ Camp Kanata $ _____
☐ Durham (Lakewood YMCA/ Downtown YMCA) $ _____
☐ Garner Road YMCA $ _____

☐ This is a **MEMORIAL GIFT**, in memory of (Print full name.) _____

METHOD OF PAYMENT (Check one.)

☐ Bill me: ☐ one time ☐ four installments

☐ Enclosed check in amount of $ _____ (payable to 2004/05 WeBuildPeople)

☐ Stock   Name of stock _____

☐ Credit card (one-time gift only):
   ☐ VISA ☐ MasterCard
   Exp. date __ / __ / __
   Card # __ __ __ __ - __ __ __ __ - __ __ __ __ - __ __ __ __

Name on card _____

TOTAL PLEDGED $ _____

AMOUNT ENCLOSED $ _____

BALANCE DUE $ _____

Amt. of pledge company will match: _____
Name of matching company: _____

☐ **SPLIT PLEDGE**
Copied: Branch _____ Date _____

DONOR'S SIGNATURE _____ DATE _____
CAMPAIGNER'S NAME (Please print.) _____

---

different. Get the personal visit if at all possible. It will serve you well in both the short and the long term.

Five things to remember as you try to get a meeting:

1. Make personal contact. Use the telephone when in doubt about other options.

2. Recruit your volunteer force in stages. Make sure to give yourself the time you need to do it well. Start early and far before the monetary part of the campaign is scheduled to begin.

3. Do everything you can to ensure that you get as personal a meeting as possible. In almost all cases, this means getting face to face with the person whom you want to be involved. For cases where your prospects are more broadly disbursed either across the country or around the world, you may have to be more creative in certain instances. Be focused on getting the meeting you want, and utilize every possible scenario available to make that happen. Offer to meet prospects at their office, home, or other setting as necessary to make it work, but try to make it a setting where either of you will be distracted. Remember that your goal is to get the meeting. Do not jeopardize getting your meeting by giving up and making your ask over the phone. I have found sentences like the following to be helpful in my calls. "I want to speak with you about a very important project that we are working on here at XYZ nonprofit organization. I will make sure not to waste your time, but it is so important that I believe it is worthy of taking the time and energy for me to come and see you personally. Can you meet on Tuesday at 9:00 or would Thursday afternoon be better for you?"

4. When it is just not possible to meet face to face, concentrate on having the most personal communication that you can. But remember, your success rate will go up the more personal you make this and other asks, so persevere on the face-to-face part of this effort.

5. Think about who you might want to bring with you to make the visit as successful as possible. Perhaps you can find someone who knows this person better than you do. If you are a staff member, bring a volunteer. If you are a volunteer, consider bringing another volunteer or staff member, as appropriate. Many things are accomplished when you do this:

- Another person meets the prospect and begins or develops a relationship.

- Having two people at the meeting shows prospects how important they are to the organization.

- One person can watch and listen to prospects while the other gauges and guides the discussion.

- One person can take written or mental notes while the other is involved in the meeting itself.

- Having two people shares the load and conversation responsibilities, allowing both individuals to learn, talk, and engage the prospect as appropriate.

- Training and experience for novice staff and volunteers.
- Your chances for getting the gift are typically even higher than if you went alone.

Likely there are even more reasons to bring additional people on an important volunteer recruitment meeting. In my experience, these meetings are among your most successful campaign asks. For your most critical solicitations and volunteer recruitment calls, having an extra person may make the difference between a yes and a not this year.

Recruitment Meeting/Ask

This is where your campaign makes its biggest step, so work hard to make this meeting as dynamic and positive as possible. If you can get the prospective volunteer to agree to work with you on the annual campaign during this meeting then you are well on your way to having a successful campaign. If you cannot get people to volunteer, very few individuals will be forced to carry the challenge of your annual support campaign goals.

Here are six tips to make the volunteer recruitment meeting go smoother and to increase your chances for success.

1. Meet and greet. When you get to the place of the meeting, introduce and make conversation as appropriate. Talk about the interests that make sense, given the situation, whether it is a fish on the wall or a picture on the desk. Take this opportunity to build the relationships.

2. Move the conversation naturally into talking about their connections with the nonprofit organization. Share stories about involvement and passion related to the organization. Make sure to get the prospect talking as much as possible while you share important relationship-building information about yourself and others in the room. Talk enthusiastically about why you are involved and passionate about the work that is done—especially the work related to the annual support campaign.

3. Talk about the annual support campaign and the need for volunteer engagement and involvement. Have the volunteer who came with you

talk about why he or she is committed and the value of the annual support campaign.

4. Remember to actively listen. The prospective volunteer will likely be sharing their stories that make them feel connected to your organization. These stories offer valuable insights into their prior involvement and provide excellent chances for relationship building. They are also likely to convince the prospect themselves on why they should get more involved!

5. Talk about the positions that you want the people to volunteer for, and why you think they personally will be a good fit for one of these positions. Use a job description to outline the job expectations.

6. Ask if they will be a volunteer as part of your annual campaign team. "If you agree to help us, know that we will be here to support you as we do this important work together. Will you help us by serving as a volunteer _____ on our annual support campaign team this year?

    a. Once you ask people to volunteer, be quiet and give them a chance to think and respond. Do not fill the silence that may occur; likely they are processing what you are asking them to do. Give them time and let them speak next!

    b. Do not apologize for asking them to be involved. Remember all of the benefits that they will receive from volunteering. A good volunteer experience is truly an exchange of benefits. Your organization receives the benefit of them helping you, and they receive the benefits of working with you.

You have done it! Respond with positive but honest answers to their concerns or questions, and do everything you can to solicit their genuine involvement. Then, whether they say yes or no, continue to the next step.

Getting Their Annual Support Gift

You have already invested time and energy in this visit. Maximizing its benefit to your nonprofit organization only makes good sense. Go ahead and make a campaign solicitation while you are there. Here are six ideas about how to make this solicitation.

1. If they have agreed to volunteer, talk about the part of the job description that explains that all campaign volunteers are asked to give a personally meaningful gift.

2. Talk about your own gift or campaign pledge and why you made it. This can show your buy-in and commitment as well as motivate the prospect to give even more.

3. Ask them to make an annual support campaign pledge. By asking them to pledge a gift over time, you raise your chances of getting a larger gift. For example, asking for a gift of $100 per month for a year gives you a $1,200 gift. For many, it is easier to ask for and get a $100-per-month gift than it is to ask for and get a $1,200 gift immediately.

4. Once you have made the ask for the gift, if possible, do not speak next. Make the ask, and then let the people think and respond before adding additional information. In the beginning, it is an uncomfortable silence for some askers, but, remember, the people you are asking are processing the information. If they need additional information at this point, let them tell you.

5. Thank them for their gift and get them to sign the pledge card. Confirm that key contact information is correct for billing and donor relationship building. Or respond to questions and concerns that they may have about their gift or the campaign itself.

6. If they need time to think about making their gift, offer to follow up rather than leaving the pledge card behind. Pledge cards left with prospects are rarely returned, and they take the control of the ask out of your hands. Offer to follow up as appropriate to get the gift. Let them know that it really is no trouble, and it is so important that you will gladly give it your time and attention.

Whenever I leave a personal volunteer recruitment meeting, I try to have a follow-up note in hand so that when I return to my car, I can fill it out right there and put it in the mail when I get back to my office. This keeps this step from getting overlooked as I return to a busy office. Writing this note immediately also keeps the meeting fresh in your mind, gets it done, and prevents you from putting the follow-up on the back burner. If part of your preparation was bringing a note card and envelope already stamped, you are halfway there!

The note does not have to be long. In today's technological world, a hand-written note sends a personal touch. One of my favorites is:

> Thank you so much for taking the time to visit with ___ and me this morning about our annual support campaign. You will make a great volunteer, and your gift will help send 12 children to summer camp next year! I appreciate your involvement more than you know, and am excited to be working closely with you. Thanks again.
>
> —**Erik**

When I get back to the office, I send out a formal letter (Exhibit 5.6) from the organization that welcomes them to the campaign. With that letter, I include the campaign calendar as well as the job description for their position. Although I have provided all this information during our meeting, sending it to them so that they receive it a couple of days later serves to remind them of what they agreed to do. This review refreshes for them their responsibilities, reinforces that they have joined our campaign ranks, and reports back to them of the forward progress of our volunteer recruitment efforts. It also shows them that we are operating the campaign in a professional way and taking it just as seriously as we do any other project at our organization. Additionally, if the first set of materials has been lost under a pile of paperwork, perhaps this set will get read!

Recruiting Basics

Start at the Top

Start at the top of your campaign volunteer teams and work your way down to the bottom. Recruit your campaign chair first and then team leaders on

EXHIBIT 5.6

Formal Letter Welcoming Volunteer

Date
Mr. Cade Barefoot
8 Vaulter's Way
Datfire, MN 27532

Dear Cade,

Thank you for agreeing to serve as a Major Gift Chair in the XYZ Nonprofit Organization's "People are the Heart of the Matter" Annual Support Campaign. Our goal is to raise $50,000 to help XYZ face the challenge of serving youth, adults, and families who might not otherwise be served unless scholarship funding is secured.

What a great opportunity to "tell the XYZ story" in our community and gain support for the work that the XYZ Organization is doing in our community!

I'm enclosing:

A copy of the Campaign Calendar

Major Gift Chair Position Description

Please begin identifying people now that you would like to visit during the campaign to share the "XYZ" story and secure their commitment of support. Bring a list of these individual's names with you to our Chair's Meeting on June 18.

Your job is simple. You need to secure four (4) Team Leaders to serve with you as we build a total volunteer organization of over 75 people to tell the XYZ story. Don't begin your recruitment yet. Our first step is to meet with all Division Chairs on June 18, 201_, share our campaign plan, clarify everyone's job, and each walk out of the meeting with the names of "Team Leader Prospects" to secure by July 23, 201_.

XYZ will provide the names of some of the people we feel would make good Team Leaders. However, please come ready to suggest who you would like to select to serve with you. Our goal is that each Division Chair will have an unduplicated, select list to contact.

Thanks again. I'll look forward to seeing you at the Division Chairs Meeting on June 18.

Sincerely,

Acelynn Grace
Chair, 201_ XYZ Annual Campaign

TIPS AND TECHNIQUES

Handling Questions and Responses

Inevitably, you will get some rejections or obstacles thrown up when you try to make an appointment or when you ask someone to help your organization during a visit. While there are many possibilities, here are a few that I have heard and some possible responses.

Some things that people might say include:

"I am too busy to meet with you, can't you just tell me over the telephone?

Say: "What we are doing is so important, it is really worth my time and yours to take the time for a meeting. I promise not to take too much of your time. Is there a time next week that we could just meet for a few minutes? I am more than willing to come to you. Would your home or office be better to meet?"

"Are you calling about the fundraising campaign? I will make a gift like I always do."

Say: "I am calling about the campaign, but I would really like to speak with you about all that is going on with it. We have some exciting new things going on, and I think that I could benefit from your ideas. Can I meet with you on Tuesday morning or would Thursday afternoon be better for you? I should only need 30 minutes or so."

"I am so committed right now that I just don't think I can take on anything else."

Say: "I would not ask you to be involved if I did not believe that you were the right person. We think so much of you at the XYZ Nonprofit Organization, and we just really believe that you are the person to do this position. Know that we will be there to help and support you in every way that we can. Would you please be _____ in our campaign? It would help so many _____."

down through your entire campaign team structure. By doing this, you make sure that you have the best possible person for each position. This topic is covered more in Chapter 6.

Set Deadlines and Timetables for Accountability

Like any other goal or objective that you plan to do, you should have timelines and a calendar for when things need to be done and by whom. Without these guidelines to help keep you moving and on track, it is unlikely that you will succeed.

Determine Who Will Be Recruited by Whom

All of your volunteers will not have the same level of ability or position of status in your community. For example, you would not want a nervous, new volunteer asking someone, who could be a major donor, but is also known to be a difficult person to deal with in conversation. You would also not want your most high-profile, community leader type volunteer asking people for $10 gifts; you would be wasting a valuable resource. Your high-caliber volunteers will have a much greater rate of success securing appointments and funds from other high-profile colleagues. It is important that you do everything possible to make sure that you get the best volunteers in your most critical positions. Organize your volunteer recruitment as much as possible so that you ensure that the highest level volunteer prospects are recruited by your best volunteer recruiters. Doing anything less risks either not getting key people to join your efforts or obtaining volunteer involvement on a level that is less than it could be.

Staff Help Volunteers Be Successful

While volunteers are doing much of the work in this campaign, staff members need to act as a strong and reliable support system. Staff members are responsible for doing everything involved in the campaign that volunteers do not do. Ensuring that all of the administrative work behind the campaign is done properly is one component. Another is making sure that volunteers are connected with viable and likely prospects. This might mean matching up more novice volunteers with prospects or donors who will build their confidence. It may also mean making sure that certain more inexperienced volunteers do not call on donors who may be particularly challenging. Your goal is to make volunteers have as positive of an experience as possible and for them to want to help year after year. Helping them to be successful ensures the best results for them and for your organization.

Monitor Volunteer Recruitment Progress Closely

Just as tracking the actual campaign dollars raised is important, so is tracking and monitoring your volunteer recruitment progress. It is imperative to this campaign that volunteers be recruited and involved. If you do not track the volunteer recruitment process, likely the process will not happen, and key people could be overlooked.

Creating a document for volunteer recruitment will serve many functions:

- A plan for who will ask whom so no one gets asked twice and no one falls through the cracks.

- A checklist for progress made and where your recruitment program stands.

- A list of people who have accepted and what positions they have accepted, so that no one is left out of future volunteer meetings and communications.

- A starting list of volunteers for next year's campaign.

 TIPS AND TECHNIQUES

Ten Tips for Building Your Recruitment Plan

❶ Whenever possible, meet and talk with people about your organization and about themselves. While this may seem simple, being intentional about building relationships is an important aspect of growing your annual support campaign and volunteer recruitment.

❷ Engage your staff and volunteer teams in getting to know people and developing relationships.

(continued)

❸ Educate your staff, volunteer groups, and board about your volunteer recruitment goals.

❹ Work with your staff and volunteers on building confidence around the function of volunteer recruitment.

❺ Make building your volunteer force a part of staff and volunteer meetings.

❻ Build a prospect list of possible volunteers on a year round basis.

❼ Visit programs and service areas of your nonprofit organization and learn who is actively involved and engaged in the work that you do.

❽ Build a timetable for recruiting a specific number of volunteers for your annual support campaign team.

❾ Once people have agreed to being a volunteer, stay in touch with them to keep them motivated and committed to the important work.

❿ Remember to keep annual support as a focus year round (with a small break after the campaign concludes!). Think both long and short term regarding whom you want involved. Remember that, over time, you will want to grow and develop your team and your fundraising goals.

Summary

The best way to involve people in the vital work that you are doing is to ask them. Being involved is good for them, and it is good for your nonprofit organization. Give your organization a chance to make a big difference by involving others in the work that you do. Share the work and spread the joy! I often think about the volunteers that I have worked with; many were asked by someone 30 or 40 years ago to get involved. After all these years, these people are still involved!

Have a specific goal in mind for your volunteer recruitment efforts. Use the diagrams in Chapter 6 to outline what your teams could look like. By recruiting and engaging volunteers in your important fundraising work, you are helping to make sure that a small handful of people don't do all the work of the annual support campaign. By getting lots of people involved, there are more people to: tell the story of your organization, build more relationships, broaden your mission, strengthen your mission work, and raise more money – all at the same time!

Think about the impact that getting someone engaged in this important work could make this year and over time. I have met and worked with people who have raised and given millions of dollars to the organizations they are serving . . . because someone asked them to get involved. Give a prospective volunteer, your community, and your organization the greatest gift of all. Ask someone to be involved with your annual support campaign!

## CHAPTER 6

Building Your Campaign Teams

After reading this chapter, you will be able to:

- Understand the annual support campaign team structure.
- Envision a team structure that will support your nonprofit.
- Identify the various components of an annual support campaign and how campaign teams help you accomplish your goals.

We now look at the overall annual support campaign team structure to see how building your annual support campaign volunteer base affects and drives your total campaign effort. In the two campaigns that are involved with a high-functioning annual support campaign (one for volunteers and one for campaign dollars), the first campaign, for volunteers, is the most critical. Once you have strong volunteer teams in place, the money will almost inevitably follow.

Team Structure

Each component of the campaign team structure has a team leader as well as team members. Every team plays an important role in communicating the organizational mission and in actually raising the charitable funds needed to accomplish the annual support campaign goals. As we discussed earlier in Chapter 5, it is important to create and recruit your team structures in order from "top down" in order to make sure that you get the best volunteers in each position. Team structures follow a few basic concepts that help to make sure that no one has more than they can handle in the overall campaign. It also helps diversify and disperse the work across a broad team of people. This helps increase the chances of overall campaign performance by making it a large group's job to tell your story and raise your annual campaign funds. In many campaigns, you will have certain areas of your campaign team structure that do more work or less work and have more or less degrees of success. By having a broad spectrum of volunteers, personalities, and demographics represented in your volunteers, you essentially are putting together a team of people who has a strong chance of success. A few key points as we build teams are:

- Recruit from the Top—start with your Campaign Chair and work downward through your volunteer organization.

- People should supervise no more than four people themselves—this helps build stronger communication, relationships, accountability and results.

- Recruit the best person possible for each position—go for your best people first and even consider recruiting the very best people for multiple year terms.

It takes many different teams to create and operate a high-functioning annual support campaign. Having separate teams working together toward a common goal divides the work of telling the story of your organization and raising the funds needed to support it. It unites the efforts of many toward a common goal with a mutual support system. This makes obtaining the goal easier to manage and achieve for both the staff and the volunteers. After looking at the key campaign leadership positions, we will look at each of the annual support campaign's components to show how to build and develop each one independently and then in succession.

Campaign Leadership

Campaign Director

In a small nonprofit organization, it is often the chief executive officer (CEO) who serves as campaign director. The campaign director's job is to make the campaign work logistically and in all manners necessary to support and enable the volunteers to be successful in their work. This means making sure that all of the processes and systems are in place to make the campaign work as efficiently as possible.

This is an extremely important staff position in the annual campaign. Often, at smaller nonprofits, the CEO has the title of annual support campaign director. At larger organizations, there may be a full-time person, other than the CEO, whose job it is to coordinate and manage the annual support campaign, or the tasks may be split among several staff members. In this second scenario, where another person (or persons) runs the annual support campaign, it is vital that the CEO show his or her full support of the campaign. If not, volunteers will get the wrong message, and key donors will see it as a less than important function in their overall giving experience to the nonprofit.

Campaign Chair

The volunteer leader of the annual campaign is the annual campaign chair. This individual should be carefully selected in order to make sure that the campaign is viewed as an important initiative in your community as well as vital to the nonprofit's operations and charitable work. By recruiting the most effective campaign chair possible, you are giving your campaign credibility and possibly influencing larger gifts toward your effort. On certain annual support campaigns that I have worked on, we have had a plan for who our campaign chair would be for up to six years in the future. This was because the level of individual that we were recruiting was the type of person who might run for a very high level government office. When you are dealing with extremely sought after individuals, it is important to recruit and cultivate them for these important positions as far ahead of time as possible.

Even if you are not dealing with such a high profile individual, it is still a good practice to cultivate and recruit these individuals years in advance when possible for several reasons. People who know that they may be future campaign chairs will likely take more note of the responsibilities of the job or consider their possible future strategy and method during the current campaign. They can also have ample time to plan for the undertaking, both from a chair perspective and from a professional perspective. It is best for the chair to have the chance to carve out the time to give your annual support campaign the focus it deserves rather than piling it on to an already busy schedule. Consider also the option of implementing a vice-chair position, a chair-in-training type of arrangement. This allows for a learning period for the incoming chair and will make for a more seamless transition from year to year. If possible or appropriate, initiate two-year terms for campaign chairs; this will allow for the first year to be a valuable learning experience, with the second year being an opportunity for even higher performance.

Do not underestimate the power of having an involved and active annual support campaign chair. Often this individual can leverage larger gifts to your campaign and sometimes can make things happen that you would never have imagined.

The first person recruited as a volunteer is the Annual Campaign Chair. Their job includes helping recruit the Major Gifts Chair, the Community Gifts Chair, the Staff Campaign Chair (as appropriate) and the Board Solicitation Chair. The top level of a high-functioning annual support team structure might look something like Exhibit 6.1.

With much larger campaigns, there may be slight variations on how the structure is developed depending on the organization and the campaign's maturity level. For example, you may have multiple Major Gift or Community Gift Co-Chairs as your campaign grows or matures. You may even have multiple Board Solicitation or Staff Campaign Co-Chairs depending on the size of your board or staff. You can also have Vice-Chairs depending on the overall size and scope of your volunteer efforts. This diagram intentionally kept the idea simplified and also supports a concept that no individual should "supervise" more than four volunteers to ensure that everyone is supported in the most effective

EXHIBIT 6.1

Annual Support Team

ways possible. For most nonprofit organizations—especially smaller ones or those embarking on their first campaign efforts—this diagram represents a very good start.

Once you have recruited your annual support campaign chair, you can evaluate who would make good chairs for each of the campaign divisions that you will be having. This would include divisions such as: staff, board, major gifts, and community gifts.

The Staff Component

By starting the campaign with your own staff, you ensure that the people who are closest to the organization's mission understand what it is that you are trying to accomplish with philanthropy. I have visited many organizations where staff members do not fundamentally understand the need for contributed dollars. Perhaps this is because they have just not been educated to the big overall picture of the organization. Often some departments or individuals within a nonprofit organization do not know about the key components of the case for support and the reason for the need for contributed funds. Sometimes these staff members work far away from or are not otherwise connected to the mission's direct impact. Although they too are contributors to the nonprofit organizations survival, they may not see firsthand how mission dollars are spent.

A typical YMCA is made up of many departments, such as child care, summer day camp, aquatics, membership, and many others. People who work as lifeguards in the indoor swimming pool likely do not understand the mission impact of the YMCA's adult fitness programs. In this case, lifeguards often think of the YMCA as the swimming pool because that is the part of the organization that they see and interact with each and every day. While they are not incorrect, they are not seeing the entire picture. Lifeguards may only see the members who use the YMCA swimming pool. They may not see the children and families and older adults whose lives are affected in other areas of the YMCA, who benefit from the YMCA and are in need of financial assistance. They might not ever see the single mother who needs to go to work and drops off her child at day camp all summer. Lifeguards may also not see that this woman could not afford such extensive and positive programming for the entire span of summer without the generosity of those who gave during the annual support campaign. Thus, this employee does not fully understand the need for contributed support.

Your organization likely has employees who perform valuable roles but do not entirely understand why your organization needs and is worthy of charitable support. These examples are numerous throughout nonprofit organizations. An informative and well-run annual support campaign helps to rectify this issue.

In addition, staff campaigns provide many other valuable by-products. An employee who works in a remote area of your organization but is well versed in the efforts of the annual support campaign feels more connected to the organization and may end up being a fabulous, well-rounded, long-term employee; but wait, there is more. That same employee may know a constituent who is connected to your organization in only one way and could be willing to become more connected.

Consider the YMCA example above. A member might only use the YMCA to come and swim at 6:00 every morning and see only the lifeguard. That one staff member may be the only link the member has to the campaign, since that employee is the only person from the YMCA that this member interacts with on a regular basis. Let us take the example one step further. Perhaps this person is a hard-to-reach CEO of a large company in your area but connects well with this staff member. Or perhaps he is a retired person with a real desire and ability to give a lot of constructive volunteer time and a sizable gift to the organization. Or perhaps he is a newcomer to the area whose private passion is one of the areas of your organization. There are many positive possibilities when we build and develop relationships with people around the annual support campaign. Staff members need to truly understanding the need and comprehend it well enough to convey it to others. If staff members are not trained to recognize and capitalize on opportunities, you may not have another chance at a potential volunteer and potential donor.

Building Your Staff Campaign

One main idea to remember is that a staff campaign should *not* be headed up by the CEO. This is because everyone in the organization on staff reports to and is accountable to this person. While the CEO may indeed get everyone to give a gift, there is a great risk that morale may suffer if people feel that they are required to give to the annual support campaign. By many people's definition, philanthropy is "joyful giving" of one's time, energy, and/or money to a given cause. If the CEO is the head of this division, you risk having people give because they are expected to give. Besides, the CEO has plenty of other work to do as the official or unofficial campaign director.

By giving someone other than the CEO or Executive Director the position of staff campaign division chair, you are achieving multiple objectives. You are preparing this other staff member for their future important fundraising work by giving them an internal constituency group to learn from and practice on. You are giving them the opportunity to learn to tell the story of your organization to people who help live this mission every day. The staff campaign chair will be responsible for making sure that every staff member hears the story of why the campaign is important, in the most personal way possible and is given the chance to make an appropriate personal gift if they so choose. This person

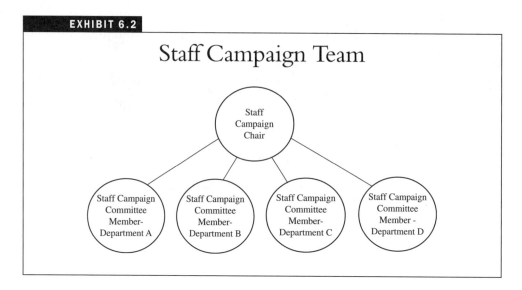

also helps to divide the work among more staff members to make sure that appropriate people are involved in the process throughout the entire staff campaign effort. Note that the staff campaign chair is not responsible for actually asking every staff member themselves. Depending on the size of the staff, this can be not only ineffective but also impractical.

Exhibits 6.2 and 6.3 show how such a campaign might happen at a 20 person nonprofit organization as each of the staff campaign committee members tells the nonprofit story and asks four employees that they do not supervise to make their personal gifts. Think about how this model could be applied to your

Things to Remember about the Staff Component of the Annual Support Campaign

- Just like any other important ask, staff members are asked face to face and as personally as is reasonable and possible.
- Staff campaigns are organized efforts with appropriate goals.
- Supervisors should never ask subordinates or direct reports for gifts as there can be implied pressure related to job performance or job security.
- All employees should hear and understand the case for support.
- Staff members should be cultivated just like any other donors or prospects to the organization.
- Staff members should be treated just like any other donors or prospects to the organization.
- Staff members should be recognized and thanked just like any other donors or prospects to the organization.

own organization. Remember that the staff campaign chair should ideally not be the executive director or the campaign director; each has enough to do on the campaign already.

It is essential that staff members understand why we are raising the money and how we plan to go about raising and spending these charitable funds. By beginning your campaign with your staff, you make sure that your team understands what you are trying to do and why you are trying to do it this way.

Board Component

One major role of the board of directors of a nonprofit organization is to make sure that the resources needed to carry out the mission exist and are made available. A highly effective way for this to occur is to have, every year, as part of the annual support campaign, an active board solicitation process that is fully participated in by the board itself.

Reasons to Have an Active
Board Solicitation

- The most committed volunteer group (your board, it is hoped) should be asked by peers. Having board members ask board members helps to get each member make a truly meaningful gift to the campaign.

- Having a personal and organized effort will generate the best fundraising results. This is as true with your board as it is with any other group of people that you will solicit.

- Many donors will ask what the board of directors gave in support of your case for giving. Full participation will reflect well on your organization. Less than 100% participation will reflect poorly. (Consider: If board members—supposedly the group of people most committed to your organization—do not contribute to this effort, others feel that perhaps they should not either.)

- Going through an active solicitation helps board members to better understand the philanthropic needs of the organization.

- As leaders of the organization, board members should make their own gifts first before asking others to support the cause.

- It gives board members the chance to practice and hone their asking skills.

- It helps board members see and understand their role in the fundraising process and that they are an important part of the overall team but the entire fundraising effort does not lie solely on their shoulders.

- It helps board members learn to tell the story of the nonprofit organization.

- It helps both board and staff members learn to run a fairly small component of the annual support campaign, see how it works, and how it is best accomplished before the rest of the campaign begins. In essence, it provides a small training ground for everyone involved in campaign management and operations.

- It helps to identify committed and less committed board members in terms of their dedication to the organization.

- It helps lead to clearer board recruitment expectations.

- It helps lead to a stronger board nomination process.

The board solicitation division does so much more than just ask your board for money in the best way possible. As outlined in the Tips and Techniques on the previous page, it also improves and engages many other practices and benefits. Your board solicitation chair is a very important position in your campaign structure. This individual not only can help you recruit other board members who will make an effective board solicitation team; he or she can also help to make effective asks of the most active and involved board members.

Exhibit 6.4 is a diagram of a board solicitation team for a board of approximately 21 people. Each of the board solicitation committee members is responsible for asking four other board members to participate in the annual support campaign through a gift and volunteer service (possibly in the major gifts or community gifts divisions, depending on the board member).

Each board solicitation committee member now has the responsibility to ask other board members to be involved in the campaign, including making a gift and participating at some level in another role in the campaign structure. These other opportunities include positions ranging from major gift division chair and community gifts campaigner/storyteller. Where board members fit into the overall campaign structure should be determined by their strengths, interests, and abilities as well as their level of overall commitment to the organization.

EXHIBIT 6.4

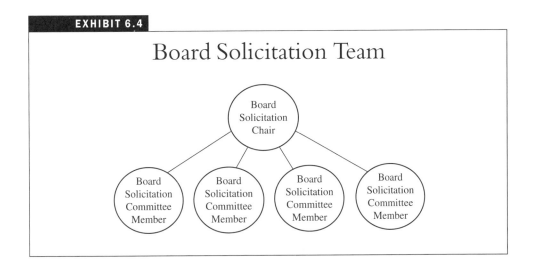

Board Solicitation Team

Major Gifts Component

A high-functioning annual support campaign has an active major gifts component. This is a group of high-capacity volunteers whose goal it is to give and get large gifts for the organization. Like any other campaign component, the major gifts team is a group of individuals with a specific goal and objective(s) around the annual support campaign effort. This group's target effort is getting the largest 10% of gifts to an organization—for most organizations, these gifts can be $1,000 or more but for some large institutions, these gifts can be $500,000 or more. Typically, this group of committed volunteers generates 50%–60% or more of the overall dollars raised for the campaign goal. It is easy to understand why this group is so important to the overall campaign success. The gift chart in Exhibit 6.5 gives you an idea of how a $250,000 annual support campaign might occur. While campaigns rarely happen exactly according to plan, it is helpful to see how an annual support campaign could happen in terms of prospects, gift amounts, and total gifts given.

As you can see from Exhibit 6.5, major gifts are a critical component of the overall annual campaign goal. It is for this reason that so much focus is given to this area. If you lose just one $25,000 gift, you will have to have an additional 1,500-plus prospects at the base level of giving (under $100) to make up for this single gift. Imagine the difference in labor and effort that it would take to ask almost 1,500 people for their gift instead of just one at $25,000! This is just another reason why asking for large and appropriate amounts is so important. If you do not obtain larger gifts in your annual support campaign efforts, it will take you much longer to achieve your goals. Without them, you may never reach your objectives.

Another aspect from this data is that, in this example, the top 54 gifts make up approximately $160,000 of the overall total. Without these major gifts, the probability that you will achieve your campaign goal remains very low. This fact makes recruiting for these major gifts volunteer positions, and managing the campaign success of these individuals, critical to the overall goal. If you do not build a strong major gifts team (see Exhibits 6.6 and 6.7), you will be left struggling to raise a large percentage of your overall annual support campaign.

EXHIBIT 6.5

Possible Breakout for a $250,000 Campaign

Gift Range in Dollars	Number of Gifts	Prospects Needed (Prospects Needed to Number of Gifts)	Total Number of Prospects	Dollars Raised in Range	Cumulative Number of Gifts	Cumulative Dollars Raised
$25,000 +	1	5 (5:1)	5	$25,000	1	$25,000
$10,000	3	15 (5:1)	20 (15 + 5)	$30,000	4 (3 + 1)	$55,000
$5,000	6	24 (4:1)	44 (20 + 24)	$30,000	10 (6 + 4)	$85,000
$2,500	12	48 (4:1)	92	$30,000	22	$115,000
$1,000	18	64 (4:1)	156	$18,000	40	$133,000
$500	54	162 (3:1)	318	$27,000	94	$160,000
$250	162	486 (3:1)	804	$40,500	256	$200,500
$100	250	750 (3:1)	1,554	$25,000	506	$225,500
Under $100	750 + –	1,500 + – (2:1)	3,054 + –	$25,000	1,256 + –	$250,500

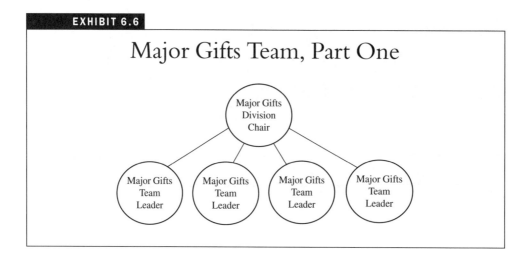

EXHIBIT 6.6

Major Gifts Team, Part One

In the next diagram, you will see how a major gift team with a goal of $15,000 might be divided. The Team Leader has an overall goal of $15,000 with each team member being asked to raise $3,000 including the Chair!). Combined with the Team Leader's personal goal of $3,000, the team raises a total of $15,000. Major gift teams do not need to all raise the same amount of money. For example, one major gifts team could have a goal of $15,000 while another may have a goal of $25,000. This is part of the art of fundraising. You want teams to stretch but you also want them to be successful. Gauge accordingly in all of your campaign efforts.

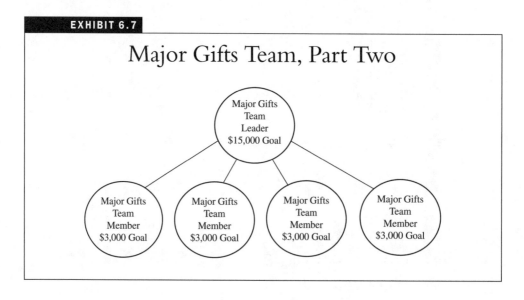

EXHIBIT 6.7

Major Gifts Team, Part Two

Community Gifts Component

The goal of the community gifts component of the annual support campaign is to involve large numbers of people to actively participate in the philanthropic process. The next section Tips and Techniques lists many of the benefits.

TIPS AND TECHNIQUES

Some Benefits of Community Gifts in your Annual Support Campaign

- Gets your constituency involved on whatever giving and volunteer participation level they are able to participate.
- Generates an owner-investor mentality among your constituency.
- Showcases your overall story/mission to your whole organization.
- Develops relationships among large groups of people.
- Encourages asking and the practice of strong financial development principles.
- Puts the emphasis on the fact that this is the organization's annual campaign effort and that everyone can play a role.
- Produces new donors.
- Gives existing donors the opportunity to upgrade their gift on an annual basis.
- Builds the fundraising volunteer base.
- Develops leadership and volunteer training opportunities.
- Helps to identify future organizational leaders.
- Gets lots of people involved in philanthropy at your organization.
- Helps build enthusiasm, excitement, and fun around the annual support campaign.

The community gifts division builds community involvement in your annual support campaign and it can pay priceless dividends in how the community perceives your nonprofit.

EXHIBIT 6.8

Community Gifts Team, Part One

In the next diagram, you will see how a community gifts team with a goal of $2,500 might be divided. One thing to remember in this diagram is that while the Team Leader has an overall goal of $2,500, each team member is asked to raise $500. Combined with the Team Leader's goal of $500, the team raises a total of $2,500. As with any of the other components such as board, staff, or major gifts, community gifts teams do not need to all raise the same amount of money. For example, one community gifts team could have a goal of $5,000 while another may have a goal of $2,500. This is part of the art of fundraising. You want teams to stretch but you also want them to be successful. Gauge accordingly in all of your campaign efforts.

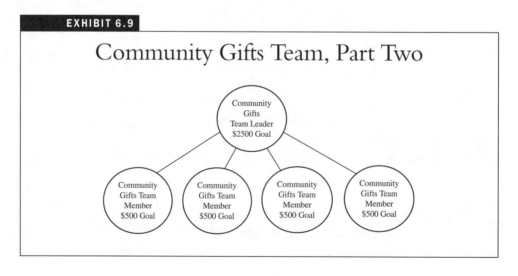

EXHIBIT 6.9

Community Gifts Team, Part Two

One of my favorite quotes about the annual support campaign is that in many cases, "Even if we did not raise any money at all, the annual support campaign would be one of the most valuable public relations and marketing efforts that we do each year." The amount of goodwill generated in the community around the annual support campaign as individuals, foundations, and corporations learn about the important work that your organization does annually can be priceless. The power of lots of people talking about the good work of your organization makes the community gifts division all the more valuable as you build and develop your annual support campaign (see Exhibits 6.8 and 6.9). While it may be tempting to pay less attention to the Community Gifts Division because of the work and effort involved in making it operate, the benefits go far beyond pledges and gifts received. The rewards of engagement and messaging along can be enough to warrant doing this important work . . . but the money is nice too!

Electronic Aspect

In today's high-tech world, an electronic component to the annual support campaign is becoming the nonprofit norm. This facet of your campaign teams can not only generate high gift and pledge yields, but it can also be a great place for people to start on their fundraising experience with your organization. By having a structured electronic and digitally focused team, you embrace a portion of philanthropic giving that is growing dramatically. You also leverage a method of asking that, when personalized, can provide a sound and structured means of raising contributed income.

The goal of your electronic team should be to connect with individuals and organizations that your annual support campaign efforts would otherwise not reach. While this means of communication and solicitation is less effective than face to face solicitation for many people, there remains a real value to this effort as it offers a way of asking people to support your organization that is very low cost and is relatively easy to accomplish. Additionally and not surprisingly, technology is a basic part of the lives of more and more people in our society. The next segment offers a glimpse at how this element might work in your organization.

IN THE REAL WORLD

As a board member for a nonprofit organization that had little organizational brand recognition, I was responsible for raising $3,000 for the annual support efforts. As a person who works across the United States, and with individuals from around the world, it did not make sense for me to solicit many of my contacts in a traditional best practice face-to-face method. Therefore, I had to use other forms of communication to make my solicitations. For many solicitations, I used the telephone but for others, I used email. I wrote up an email that outlined my goals and objectives, as well as where the funds would be utilized—followed, by an ask for a specific amount of money. I personalized each note; it was from me to the recipient with whom I had an existing and positive relationship.

After sending out approximately 25 of these emails and asking my geographically close connections in more personal ways, I had raised over $1,500. My emails raised just over half of my $3,000 goal, leaving approximately $1,500 to raise through more traditional fundraising techniques. I raised the remainder of the money with just a couple of more personal asks.

Just because this division happens to be electronic in nature is no reason that it should not be developed with the same intentionality that the rest of the parts of staff, board, major gifts, and community gifts divisions are developed. It is an important developmental and communication tool that is worthy of being organized, managed, and accounted for in the same ways that the other divisions are.

Here is an example of an email that I sent out that raised over $1,500 from approximately 25 asks (from the previous In the Real World example). I include this example to show how such an email might be written as well as to show how easy it might be for volunteers to do email solicitations for your organization! Continue to remember that face to face is the most effective way to solicit whenever possible, but email or other direct messaging methods may be the most effective method for certain situations.

> I need your help to change the world. Every day almost 16,000 children die from hunger-related causes—one child every five seconds.
>
> I work with a group of students, and serve on the Board of Advisors, to an organization called Nourish International. Nourish International works with college students to design and implement long-term solutions to eradicate poverty and hunger worldwide. By collaborating with other nonprofits on the

international stage, Nourish International is changing the world—one student, one community, one child at a time.

Worldwide, more than 1 billion people live below the international poverty line, earning less than $1 per day.

My goal in this initiative is to draw attention to the challenge of world hunger AND to make a small difference in it. This is where you come in. I need your help to make this change possible. I need your help to contribute funds to make positive change happen. I need your help to raise funds to help combat this worldwide epidemic. I need your help to support the 501 c3 charity—Nourish International.

820 million people in the developing world are undernourished—almost six million children under the age of 5 die every year as a result of hunger.

If you are willing to help me help others through Nourish International, just respond to this email and let me know the level of support that you can offer. I am asking if you could help make this year a less hungry one for a child by participating with a gift of $50 or even more if you can. Please let me know what amount by February 28, 201_, and I will make arrangements to provide this special gift to Nourish International. My goal is to raise at least $3,000 to help college students engage in world hunger–related projects—100% of all gifts help Nourish International meet that objective. Thanks again for anything you can do.

A common mistake made by nonprofit organizations who embrace an electronic/digital component (or telephone component, as discussed next) is that everyone uses these methods of asking for every solicitation. Since it is not face to face, making asks in this way is often viewed as less time consuming, less risky, less complicated, and less cumbersome for volunteers. While this may all be true, this method is also often less effective. In my own personal example presented in the "In the Real World" section, I raised approximately half of the funds through the electronic/digital methods. At the same time, I made far fewer asks in a face-to-face method—yet they raised approximately the same amount of dollars. I utilized the electronic method of making a solicitation (in my case, email) for individuals with whom it was virtually impossible and certainly highly impractical to make face-to-face solicitations. For the individuals with whom it was possible and practical, I made personal face-to-face solicitations. As I anticipated, these generated larger gift amounts to the nonprofit.

Email and text messaging—when used judiciously and with the right audience—can be a very productive means of fundraising. These methods can be especially effective for use with fundraising volunteers who are more resistant to or are truly uncomfortable (not just uneasy to begin with) at making face-to-face solicitations.

Remember also that one reason to have these additional campaign components (telephone, digital, electronic, etc.) is to allow campaign volunteers to participate in the solicitation process even if they are not good face to face askers or are not yet ready to perform face to face solicitations because of a lack of confidence, personal ability, etc.. The goal of any good telephone, digital, or email aspect of an annual support campaign is not to undermine or utilize less effective methods of solicitation or to utilize a one-size-fits-all approach. Indeed, it is just the opposite. The goal with any campaign is to approach as many donors with as personal a solicitation as possible. When utilized properly, the electronic/digital division and the telephone component expand and enhance your reach to build a comprehensive and cohesive overall annual support campaign.

One strategy that many nonprofits use in collaboration with their electronic and digital efforts is to utilize a "Donate Now" type button on their Web sites. This button, on its own, throughout the year will typically not generate many if any donations. During a campaign, this button can be linked in digital communications and in certain circumstances be a useful tool. For example, an e-mail sent to a colleague in a distant location can provide a link to a nonprofit's Web site and an ability to make a contribution immediately. This allows the entire transaction to take place electronically; no need to take the extra step of waiting for a check in the mail that the sender might forget to write. This approach can be viewed being used effectively in any number of online nonprofit venues. Just do a search under "nonprofit" and "donate now" and you will find seemingly countless examples of online giving options.

Another way that this tactic is being played out is through the development of personal web pages for fundraising efforts on the Internet. You will see this strategy being carried out across the country and around the world. People are now creating personal web pages specifically for fundraising efforts to which they direct their electronic contacts through various Internet platforms. Using one or both of these strategies can assist in raising more of these community gifts contributions for your organization. Again, an interesting exercise to do here is to put in "fundraising" and "personal web page" into a search engine. You will see many platforms and examples with just a little bit of research.

Do not be lulled into thinking that because this division is more automated in nature that it is any less significant. It is not. By its nature, this division is able to make many, many, more asks of possible donors and donor/prospects. This fact alone would drive the need for accountability and management, not withstanding the fact that it is a team unto itself and needs to be quantified as such. At the same time, however, do not think that electronic or digital efforts alone will make your campaign successful. These community gifts aspects can be very successful in certain populations and in certain applications but they are not likely to be your highest producing method of fundraising unless you are a truly exceptional organization with very high visibility in the marketplace. Even then, it will take a great deal of focus and intentionality for it to be as successful as it can be.

Exhibit 6.10 shows how the electronic/digital aspects of the annual campaign falls under the leadership of the Community Gifts Division. Each effort should have a Team Leader and a dedicated group of volunteers to initiate and carry out the efforts as appropriate. Each effort should also have specific goals and objectives that support the overall campaign goals.

EXHIBIT 6.10

Community Gifts Division

Telephone Aspect

The telephone is the medium that regularly comes to mind when people think of annual support campaigns. Many of us receive our yearly phone call for support from our alma maters, since colleges and universities often utilize phone-a-thons as part of their annual support campaigns.

While I agree that the telephone can be a powerful tool for raising annual support contributions in certain circumstances, it should be used appropriately within the context of your overall annual campaign strategy. Optimally, the telephone should almost never be used in soliciting people whose gifts are in the top 10% of your overall pool of donors and prospects to your annual campaign. Donors who have the potential to give major gifts should be contacted in a more personal way as it will lead to higher gifts being made and the story being told in a more personal way. Donors who have the potential to give major gifts should be contacted through your major gifts teams rather than through a less effective method of solicitation. In this way, the most personal ask is made which will ultimately increase your chances of obtaining the best possible gift from the individual donor.

Imagine that you are one of a nonprofit organization's largest donors. You are contacted by telephone by someone who does not properly pronounce your name. What impression of the nonprofit would you have? Would you feel valued and appreciated? Or would you feel as if the nonprofit organization did not really appreciate you as they should? Or imagine that a potentially high-dollar donor gets a phone-a-thon call and gives $250. The volunteer might be thrilled at the amount of the gift, never knowing that this donor had the potential to give $25,000 or more. For this reason and many more, telephone and all electronic solicitations in the annual support campaign should be carefully screened and vetted prior to the contacts being made. As the examples provided reveal, contacting top prospects with a less personal ask can have real consequences.

Now that we have established that the telephone can be a useful tool but that it should not be the basis for every ask in your annual support campaign, let us look at a few techniques that can make your telephone efforts more productive.

- *Have a plan.* It is important that you have a plan for whom to call, when to call, where to call, why to call, and how to call. Whatever human resources you utilize, have a plan for how to measure, train, and monitor their performance.

- *Make telephoning fun.* Make sure that your telephone callers have energy and enthusiasm. Have contests, fun themes or other creative, uplifting ideas to motivate callers to continue through the nos and celebrate the yeses.

- *Make sure that your information is good.* Work hard not to give callers bad addresses and phone numbers, as it is demoralizing to get no answers or disconnected messages when you are giving your time and energy to a cause that you care about. Explain that no list is perfect before you begin, but do everything possible to have your information as complete and accurate as possible prior to beginning your calling efforts.

- *Invest in this aspect of your annual support campaign just as you would any other.* Providing resources, training, volunteers, and staff as appropriate will help to make the best possible outcome.

- *When talking to people on the telephone, make sure that they are all treated with the dignity and respect that they deserve.* If they are on your list to call, they are an important or potentially very important person. Know that each call is both a solicitation for today and a cultivation for tomorrow. Make kindness and respect a part of every call.

The telephone can be a great way to generate new gifts, but it is also a tremendous way to thank donors for their prior gifts. Many nonprofits are now utilizing the telephone to create and develop "thank-you-thons" that allow volunteers to contact previous and existing donors, not to solicit funds, but to thank them for their participation and update them on how their funds are being used. Donors are pleasantly surprised that they are contacted just to be thanked; this can be one more layer in the cultivation and maturation process of your donors and of your volunteers.

Thus, the telephone can be a sound technique for soliciting and developing gift prospects as part of the campaign. The telephone portion is a good way to manage smaller gift donors and is an obvious choice in geographically remote areas of the country or when your donor base is geographically scattered around the country or across the globe.

Telemarketing, or telefundraising, as it has sometimes been called, can:

- Generate donor or prospect leads.
- Retain existing donors with regular contact.
- Obtain and update donor and prospect information.

Different types of phone activities might include:

- Single gift calls for new, current, or lapsed donors.
- Monthly sponsorship calls for getting donors to sponsor specific organizational initiatives.
- Thank-you calls for donors.
- Event follow-up calls.
- Donor relations calls providing information, such as reporting to donors about how their gifts have been used or how progress is being made related to special projects.

As we discussed, telemarketing activities have been found to be best when they are integrated into an overall fundraising and communications plan. That means that they:

- Align with a donor relationship management program.
- Coordinate with all other solicitations.
- Facilitate donor dialogue and suggestions.
- Provide donor acknowledgment and updates for successful campaigns and programs.

Phone-a-thons are typically best performed when the constituency that you are trying to solicit is most likely to pick up the phone. Because the world of telecommunications is changing quickly, this timing concern may become less of an issue as potential donor prospects more and more often carry their phone with them at all times. However, at the time of this writing, landline telephones still play an active role in the lives of many households. If you are dealing with a population or country where landline telephones are less common, the timing of the calls should be made so that the person you are calling is most likely to be able to pick up the phone, take the time to listen and engage in a conversation, and then ultimately agree to make a gift. For the purpose of the following script, it is assumed that this occurs in the evening.

XYZ Nonprofit Organization Phone-a-thon Script

Hi, is _____ at home tonight?

This is _____, and I'm a *volunteer* calling from the XYZ Nonprofit Organization annual phone-a-thon for sustaining support. I understand that you or your family has had a history with XYZ Nonprofit Organization . . . when were you last there?

XYZ Nonprofit Organization means an awful lot to me, and that is why I am volunteering here tonight.

Have you had a chance to see the brochure that we sent out describing our fundraising effort? (If a brochure has been sent out.)

Well, our annual campaign goal is $50,000 this year. And most of that goes directly to _____ for _____ so that they can _____.

We're also raising money for other efforts as well.

Would you consider a making gift in the range of $_____? (Ask for *at least* $100!)

That's great! Thank you from all of us here tonight and also from all the _____ who you will be helping. Can I just make sure that your contact information is correct?

Thank you for your time and I hope that you and your family sleep well knowing you helped a _____ with your generous gift. Have a great rest of the day!

XYZ Nonprofit Organization Phone-a-thon Training

Tips for Success

- Make your own pledge first. The bigger you make it, the more you will be able to ask others to pledge.

- Have a *smile* in your voice so people will be happy to talk with you.

- Let people know that you are a *volunteer*!

- Engage people by asking them about their XYZ Nonprofit Organization experience.

- Ask for a specific amount (at least $100).

- Make lots of calls. Do not talk to answering machines; it takes time from other contacts.

Don't Forget!

- Have a *smile* in your voice.

- Realize that you are doing people a favor by making these calls.
  - First, _____ is happening because you are taking the time to make these phone calls.
  - Second, we will make the donor feel great when we thank them, several times, for the act of kindness their gift produces.

- Call your friends, cousins, grandparents, and the like to get warmed up. Long-distance calls are fine—just do not allow any one call to get too long.

- Use the script to get started but feel free to share your own XYZ Non-profit experiences as appropriate.

- How is the person you are calling related to the nonprofit organization? Does the person's age or occupation suggest that he or she could give more than $100? If yes, ask the person to sponsor something specific. Have a list of sponsor levels available for your call makers as it really helps donors to see and understand where the money will go. For example:

Sponsor levels for an Animal Rescue Center might be:

- $150 = 1 animal for 1 month
- $250 = 1 animal for 1 month + food for 1 month
- $350 = 1 animal for 1 month + food + base line medical care
- Etc.

- Make *lots* of calls. The more people you call, the more will say *yes*.
- Think like a professional salesperson for just these couple of hours. Dial the number and read the form while it is ringing.
- Fill out the form while you are on the phone with the person. If no one answers after five rings, hang up and try again later.
- If you get an answering machine, hang up and try again later.
- Every time you get a *yes,* let the phone-a-thon leadership and everyone else know. It is exciting for you, the donor, and others in the room to know your success. Even the other call recipients may hear the cheers; they will hear that this is a fun and successful endeavor in which they should give and participate.
- Phone-a-thon leadership should come and pick up your cards every few minutes and there should be some prizes too!
- Keep calling and sharing your successes!

Summary

Building campaign teams with spirit and commitment leads to higher functioning and more successful annual support campaigns. If you focus your efforts to building stronger, more complete volunteer teams, when it comes time to raise the charitable funds that you need, you will have a group of dedicated people to help you complete the task at hand. If you do not recruit and build strong and well developed campaign teams, then when it comes time to raise the money, you will be more alone than you should be. Many hands make light work—the annual campaign is no different than any other large programming initiative.

Each division of the campaign plays an important role in the overall effort. The staff component gives staff the opportunity to give while at the same time educating them about all of the great work that your nonprofit is doing in the community. The board component gives your board the opportunity to learn and practice storytelling as well as asking for the gift on an annual basis. The major gifts division focuses on raising the larger campaign gifts that likely will be necessary to make your overall campaign goal while the Community Gifts Division focuses on giving everyone in your community the chance to support the campaign goals and give something to your organization.

Remember that if you want to succeed in annual support, you need to have two focused campaign efforts. If you put time, energy, attention, focus, and re-sources into the first campaign to recruit volunteers, then raising the money will be easier than you might expect. Without volunteers, we are destined to underperform and underachieve in our fundraising efforts.

## CHAPTER 7

Building Relationships and Asking for the Gift

After reading this chapter, you will be able to:

- Implement a donor cultivation program at your organization.
- Be more prepared to ask for the the gift.
- Realize the need to acknowledge and thank donors and establish ways to do it.

Building Relationships and Cultivating Donors

There is no way around it—building relationships is a key ingredient in the annual campaign mix. In Chapter 5, we addressed the merit of building relationships as it relates to recruiting volunteers. The same principles are at work with cultivating donors. When you have an existing solid relationship with the people whom you will eventually ask for a donation, your solicitation will almost always go significantly more smoothly than if you had no relationship at all. Bringing community members closer to your organization and building relationships with them is positive in so many ways. There are many benefits for the volunteer themselves such as: being part of something bigger than themselves, learning about another aspect of their community, sharing skills in an arena that they enjoy, forming new or deepening existing friendships, feeling like they are making a difference in their community or the world and so on. Your organization benefits from these healthy relationships by having more people to help: educate the community about your organizational mission, make your nonprofit operate, meet the challenges facing your nonprofit, raise charitable funds, and so on.

The cliché no man is an island is true for nonprofits as well. Nonprofits cannot do it alone, nor are they better served by doing so. There is much to be gained from the larger community getting involved in the superb and necessary work that they are doing. Build the relationships for the strength of the organization, for the betterment of those who benefit from your mission, for the fulfillment of the volunteers and for your community as a whole.

Remember that one of our goals is to have the communities that we serve fundamentally understand the work that we are doing and become a part of making that work happen on a regular basis. We want our constituency to absorb our missions and be willing to assist in and fund the challenges that we face. We want to bring people of affluence and influence closer to our nonprofit organization so that we can grow and sustain our work.

In order for our constituency to understand us, we must first work to understand them. What about our mission speaks most to them? What about our mission motivates them to be most engaged and involved? What in their own lives makes them want to be involved with us as an organization? These and so many other questions will lead us to realize what compels donors and how we can best connect with them both personally and professionally.

If cultivation is done correctly, there will be many individuals in our community who will be able to articulate our nonprofit organization's mission with passion, and have influence on decisions at meetings, government agencies, businesses, and civic institutions. These same people will not only help us to implement a successful annual campaign program but also identify areas for program expansion, help us build an enviable community outreach program, and help us to be in an excellent position to raise significant funding for capital initiatives or other financial development objectives that we may have in the years to come. Donor cultivation can be a tremendous way of connecting and engaging people in the work we do . . . so what is it and what does it look like?

Do You Know Them as Well as You Should?

If I was to come up to you and ask you for $1 million, never having met you, what would you think and feel? I find it interesting that so many of our non-profit organizations wonder why major donors are not willing to give them large gifts when the nonprofit is not willing to take the time to truly get to know donors and their interests. This concept epitomizes cultivation; the key is to develop a solid, personal relationship with your major gifts prospects. By knowing your major gifts prospects as if they are your best friends, you will come to know the many nuances of their lives that will ultimately lead to heightened potential for a major gift. They will become the best friends of your nonprofit.

Exercise

"How Well Do You Know Them . . . Really?"

Review the information list. Put a check mark next to every category you can answer about one of your best friends.

Your Best Friend's..

Birthday _____

Age _____

Children's Names_____

Children's Ages _____

About how much debt they have_____

(continued)

(continued)

The place they call "home" _____

Pet's name _____

High school name and or/location _____

How they met their spouse (if applicable) _____

Top 3 favorite charities/causes _____

Properties (homes, land, business, etc,) they own_____

Cell phone number _____

Threshold for what a large contribution to a charity would be for them

_____

Income—where it comes from and about how much it is _____

Other very close friend's name_____

Favorite things to do on the weekend _____

Now review the information list. Put a check mark next to every category you can answer about one of your very top prospects.

Your Very Top Campaign Prospect's . . .

Birthday_____

Age _____

Children's Names_____

Children's Ages _____

About how much debt they have_____

The place they call "home" _____

Pet's name _____

High school name and or/location _____

How they met their spouse (if applicable) _____

Top 3 favorite charities/causes _____

Properties (homes, land, business, etc,) they own_____

(continued)

Cell phone number _____

Threshold for what a large contribution to a charity would be _____

Income—where it comes from and about how much it is _____

Other very close friend's name_____

Favorite things to do on the weekend _____

The goal of this exercise is to show how well we should consider knowing our prospects prior to making a significant solicitation.

Another way to look at donor cultivation is to recognize that people give at the level where their passion for your organization matches their ability to give. By this, I mean that people will make their charitable gift where their concern and empathy for the work you do intersects with their ability to make a gift.

So . . . if you can get people's interest and passion to grow in your organization and the work that you are doing, their gift will almost always grow proportionately. We cannot control what people earn or have as assets, but we can control how much they know about us and the work that we do. This is where good development work happens and annual support campaign giving becomes such comprehensive work.

Think about cultivation as a year-round process that focuses:

- *Mostly* on information gathering and growing closer to the prospect.

- *Some* on thanking and reporting information to the individual . . . and this does not have to be just thanking for money!

- And *only occasionally* asking for a gift.

Based on the idea that cultivation is a year round process that eventually leads to a gift of financial support, our objective is *not* to meet with people just for the sake of meeting with them. Our meetings and conversations should have a specific purpose in mind, beginning simply with gathering identifying information about them and their interests in our organizational work. Even casual, chance interactions can further relationship-building efforts. By getting to know your donors as individuals and friends, you ultimately will identify the values and interests that are important to them. This knowledge is what will most likely lead you to a major gift—whether in your annual support campaign or some other worthwhile fundraising endeavor.

During this period, you will also be developing a relationship of trust and mutual respect, which will lead to confidence in and between both parties. ("I will give you a pledge because I trust and respect you," and "I trust that you will pay your pledge because I trust and respect you.") Loyalty grows over time and is a function of involvement and ownership. Think of it as a ladder upon which each step is a level of commitment that deepens and grows based on the previous step.

It is worth noting here that before a cultivation plan can be fully implemented, those who will be involved in working with prospects should attend a thorough orientation on your organizational story. In addition, a prospect profile should be developed. Sample information for this type of profile is outlined later in this chapter.

Your ultimate goal should be to bring your prospects and donors closer to your organization at every logical and possible opportunity. To exemplify this, think of the items in the bulleted list as a ladder going from bottom to top. While there are certainly additional or other steps that could be added, the example gives you an idea of how relationships develop over time and are built on strong foundations. When people do each step, it brings them a bit closer to your nonprofit.

 TIPS AND TECHNIQUES

Key Points to Remember

- The simplest things can often make a *huge* difference.
- Personal contacts, written communication, events, and activities all bring prospects closer to you.
- Track and monitor your ongoing progress carefully, effectively, and confidentially.

Top of the Ladder (read from bottom to top for full effect)

▲ Gives even larger gifts!

▲ Takes on deeper volunteer assignments and challenges.

▲ Makes a gift of money to your organization.

▲ Forms and keeps deep relationships with other volunteers, program participants, or staff at your nonprofit.

▲ Volunteers for one of your programs or initiatives.

▲ Continues nonprofit program participation.

▲ Becomes a part of a small community at your nonprofit.

▲ Participates in a program that you provide.

▲ First learns about your organization.

Bottom of the Ladder

These steps do not necessarily happen exactly as outlined, but it is interesting to see how donor engagement can and might progress at your nonprofit organization.

It is important to remember that loyalty grows through involvement over time. Continuously try to engage people and make them "co-owners" whenever possible.

The Donor Cultivation Process

No one has time to cultivate and get to know every possible prospect in the same way. Well organized financial development programs typically divide potential donors and prospects into categories. The Donor Cultivation Process in this section shows one method of dividing and categorizing your donor base into a logical and progressive system. It also brings clarity and focus to an otherwise large group of people so that your efforts have more focused direction and purpose. For some organizations, the following example's total prospect numbers will be too few and for other organizations, the number of prospects will be too many. The point here is that you should have select groups and individuals on which to focus your time and attention in order to obtain the best results.

Choose a number that is right for you or your team members, and stick to it. If you make the process work well your efforts will bear great fruit.

You should strongly consider dividing your donor prospects into three distinct groups:

The Top 15. The first group consists of people who have both the capacity and the possibility for interest in giving to your programs or service. This group is a highly selective group of approximately 15 people whom you believe are likely to give major gifts with proper cultivation. This is where you will spend most of your time and personal energy.

The Second 30. This group contains replacements who will take the place of anyone who falls out of the Top 15 during the cultivation and ultimately the solicitation process. This means that you always have at least 15 people in the first group; when one of them falls out of this group for any reason, someone from the Second 30 can rise immediately into the Top 15. You will meet with members of this group in small group settings to continue to learn about them and grow relationships. You should plan to spend less one-on-one time with this group than with the Top 15.

Everyone Else! The third group is everyone else. This is the group that you are constantly looking at and learning about, to see if someone is a better fit for either of the two previous groups. This group receives less individual attention but is always on your radar. You spend time here chatting and assessing, ear to the ground and aware.

Where Do We Look for Prospects?

In forming your nonprofit organization's cultivation program plan, there are three significant areas that are obvious places to look:

1. Program Leaders

Program leaders often come from program participants who believe in the nonprofit organization's mission and demonstrate a passion for the endeavors.

2. Board and Committee Leaders

Individuals targeted as prospects may come from members, program participants, or from other leadership areas within your community. Board and committee leaders are likely prospects because of their passion and belief in your organization and its mission. Individuals who may fit this profile often come from positions in your community such as banking, real estate, city or county government, or top level business leaders from other industries.

3. Past or Current Donors

Gifts come from all areas of your community. If you analyze this group, you will see some people that are more capable of giving larger gifts. Many in this category will also be capable of soliciting additional support from others as well. Because they already have a belief in the work that you are doing, this group can become highly engaged and strong contributors if properly cultivated.

Each of these areas, whether philanthropic, government or program related, can be an entry point in developing volunteers for the other areas. For example, a nonprofit volunteer who is a vice president for an influential business in the community may be a prime candidate for further cultivation. This person could become a member of a program committee, move to the board of advisors, serve as a team leader or chair in your annual support campaign, or become the lead solicitor for major gifts.

Other groups to consider:

- People who have given $5,000 or more to your organization (or a large gift to your nonprofit — whatever that means to you).
- People who have given $500 (or other proportionately large gift to your organization) or more annually to your organization but you know little or nothing about
- Foundation board members who might be connected or connectable to your nonprofit
- Your endowment donors
- Other groups

Key Points to Remember

- Spend the most time with prospects who offer the most potential (Top 15 and Second 30).
- Set clear priorities.
- You cannot do everything all of the time. Consider what is the greatest return on your investment of time right now.
- Focus on getting to know people well, not on immediately making a solicitation or ask.

Questions to consider when looking for larger gift prospects:

- Who are the five wealthiest members of your board?
- Who are the five wealthiest people associated with your nonprofit in general?
- Who are the five most influential "power people" in your service area?
- What family foundation or company foundations are in your service area?
- Which people in your organization love it the most?
- Which individuals have given over longest period to your organization?
- Which individuals have given the most money to you over the last five years?

Questions to consider when looking for larger gift prospects, if you have done an annual support campaign before:

- Who were the five wealthiest individual contributors?
- Who were the five largest contributors?
- Who were the five largest corporate contributors?
- Who were the decision makers at each company just listed?
- Which individuals have given the longest?
- Which individuals have given the most over the last five years?

Because your cultivation efforts can help you to raise more large gifts (and remember that your top 10% of gifts will likely make up close to 60% of your overall campaign goal), it is important to bring focus to this area. A system of cultivating donors like the one outlined here can help you for many reasons.

- It can help you raise more money.

- It involves key community leaders in your efforts.

- It gets your organization's story into different and influential parts of the community.

- It can provide a valuable source of future resources to your nonprofit (board members, volunteers, campaign leaders, etc.).

- It can help to raise people's sights for larger gifts.

What Do I Learn through Cultivation and Relationship Building?

Through cultivation and relationship building, we want to be sure that each prospect knows and understands our nonprofit organization's story and our vision for the future. At the same time, we want to learn the prospect's story and vision for the future. A good place to start the process is to think about the things that you know and do not know about your prospect. The next pages outline some things you should consider learning about your donor/prospects.

Primary Information

1. Name (s)

2. Primary address

3. Secondary address

4. Office address

5. Contact numbers

    a. Home

    b. Office

    c. Cell phone

    d. Fax

6. Email addresses

    a. Home

    b. Office

7. Preferred Method of Communication

    Email, text message, telephone, face to face, other

Relationship to the Nonprofit

1. Total giving to the organization, including last gift

2. Largest gift and purpose

3. Past solicitation results

4. Estimated capacity for giving

5. Estimated likely gift

6. Existing links to your nonprofit

7. Board service, volunteer service, years of service with your nonprofit

8. Positions held

9. Best persons to "cultivate" them—think of both staff and volunteer names

Professional Information

1. Profession

2. Company information (background, company foundation, web address, etc.)

3. Professional memberships, clubs associations, etc.

4. Other?

Personal Information

1. Age

2. Birthday

3. Where they grew up/call "home"

4. Schools/Degrees

5. Awards/Honors

6. Family information

7. Spouse information (profession, etc.)

8. Number of children (Ages, schools)

9. Parents and other relatives of interest

10. Pets

11. Hobbies and interests

12. Travel interests

13. Nonprofit organizational program interests

Assets

1. Sources of money/income/wealth

2. Annual income (projection)

3. Stock and/or bond holdings

4. Principal home value

5. Value of other homes/real estate holdings

6. Family foundations

7. Other assets

8. Have they made their will/estate plan?

9. Other planned gifts known

10. Estimated net worth

Community Information

1. Contributions to other organizations

2. Other board or officer positions held

3. Activities of involvement

4. Political affiliation/involvement

Evaluations to Be Made by Your Organization

1. Gift potential

2. Ranking codes (A, B, C, etc.) (See Exhibit 7.1).

3. Outright gift or deferred?

4. Timing

5. Cultivator/campaigner assigned

6. Date of assignment (for the solicitation)

7. Date due for results (for the ask)

This is a lot of information, and likely you will never learn all of these details for some people. The information does, however, help to frame out how well you really know the people you will be asking for money.

How Do I Cultivate Donors and Prospects?

When cultivating donors and prospects, use every opportunity possible to deepen and strengthen the relationships that you have with them. Since some key aspects of loyalty are engagement and involvement, keep your donors and prospects involved in what your organization is doing! This may mean everything from getting them to come to one of your programs, to just taking time to connect with them and what is going on in their lives. You should try to meet, write, or call your prospects in an effort to stay in touch without being annoying. You do not want them to feel as if you are pursuing them aggressively, just that you want to have a friendly and professional relationship with them. When in doubt, take the opportunity to connect. This means writing the extra note, sending the card, taking the time to chat, inviting them to a nonprofit gathering, and the like. It is important to note at this point that research cannot replace relationship building in the process. The fuller, more sincere and solid the relationships, the better your chances of attaining a positive outcome when it is time to make the ask.

Good cultivation is done in accordance with targeted strategies specifically designed for each individual prospective donor. Each donor cultivation effort begins by identifying the desired outcome with the prospective donor. What gift do we hope to achieve at the culmination of our efforts at this point? It also provides a plan of the steps that are needed to bring the cultivation efforts to the desired outcome. What do we need to do to bring this prospective donor closer to our organization and to making a larger gift? A good cultivation process also identifies the best people (volunteer and/or staff) to take the responsibility of completing the cultivation work and ultimately to ask for the gift. Who are the best people to have involved in this relationship? Once all of this information is put into place, a timeline for the cultivation effort is developed, implemented, and reviewed on a regular basis.

Implementing the Cultivation Process

Donor cultivation occurs in several ways: individual meetings (general or targeted) with prospects, cultivation events, nonprofit organization tours, boards of advisors and committee meetings, lobby displays, newsletters, programs and/or fundraising videos, and so on. Each of these strategies must be developed, keeping in mind whether it is for general information/education or aimed at a specific individual or audience.

Once an individual cultivation activity is decided on, it should be scripted and very well planned whenever possible. This preparation will provide those individuals who will be in charge of the activity with talking points to use and what to focus on during the meeting/cultivation effort.

Another way of looking at cultivation is to move each prospect along the donor cultivation ranking scale in Exhibit 7.1

EXHIBIT 7.1		
Donor Cultivation Ranking Scale		
Status	**Translation**	**Ranking**
Passionate	They share the dream and vision for the organization	A
Some Interest	They are interested in your organization	B
Awareness	They know who you are as an organization	C

When a prospect achieves an A ranking, it is possibly/probably time to ask him or her to consider making a significant gift to your organization.

The goal should be to identify and take each of your best prospects from where they are now—whether as an A, B or C ranking—to a place where they are prepared to participate even more fully in your organization.

Ultimately, with every major gift prospect, we want to identify:

- What phase of cultivation is the person, A, B, or C?

- Who is the best person to ask the person and get him involved?

- An individualized approach that focuses on the donor/prospect's interests.

- How to move them closer to our organization. This means strategizing with the lead person on each visit (who is that person?) and having a clear, agreed-on course of action prior to each meeting.

- Each cultivation visit should bring further clarity to these questions:

  - Who should ultimately make the ask?

  - What specifically are we going to ask them for? (a gift, campaign assistance such as chair, leader, volunteer, etc.)?

  - How much should we request?

  - Where should we ask them?

  - When is the best time to make the ask?

Once you feel confident that your prospects are well cultivated and that you know the answers to these questions, you are ready to ask for a major gift. As described in Exhibit 7.1, that prospect will hopefully be ranked as an A. If you move people through the process too quickly, you will not get as good results as if you moved the through the process more effectively. Rushing through donor cultivation may lead to donors giving less than their potential.

Some points to consider as you progress:

- Make your prospect objectives as clear and concise as possible.

- Do not make your prospect objectives unrealistic, but do not settle for less than great results.

- Do not rush the cultivation process and get a premature no.
- Remember to focus on learning about prospects' interests during cultivation. Do not jump too quickly to the close. Learn the needs, desires, and values of prospects as they relate to your nonprofit. Then, and only then, ask them to make a significant gift.
- There is little substitution for *personal* communication.
- Center your connection to prospects on them and on your organizational mission.

Once you have gathered information about prospects and ranked them, you are ready to begin tracking their progress using a donor and prospect cultivation management tracking program or tool.

The donor and prospect cultivation management tracking form (see Exhibit 7.2) is used so that all parties involved with prospects have a clear understanding of where each prospect is on the donor cultivation ranking scale, what step has just occurred, and what the next step is. Optimally, the form is reviewed and updated no less than once per month, which keeps the information accurate and available for all who need it. This document is usually kept by the campaign director or other administrative staff person. Staff and volunteers contact them as appropriate to manage and update the information.

Two critical aspects of the entire cultivation process are confidentiality and the importance of regular attention to your top prospects. By keeping these two fundamental ideas in mind, you will have much success and fewer negative outcomes.

The tracking form in Exhibit 7.2 gives you an idea of how to track donor and prospect engagement and the next steps for your annual support campaign.

Ways to Cultivate Donors and Relationships

Every time we come in contact with people associated with our organization or leaders in the community, we can build relationships with them. It can be as simple as a chance meeting at your organization or at the grocery

Donor and Prospect Cultivation Tracking Form/Template

Name	Involvement	Staff Assigned	Volunteer Assigned	Area of Interest	Gift Target	Prospect Readiness (A–C)*	Next Move	Date	Expected Outcome
1. Betty Haswell	Parent of Participant	George Babish	Dan Mirolli	Children's Programs	$2,500	A	Dan contact to set up meeting at Child Care Site to make solicitation	Sept 1, 20___	Gift & chair community gifts
2. Thad Gifford-Smith	Program participant 3 times per week	Calvin Allen	Eric Guajardo	Homeless Shelter	$5,000	C	Eric invite to coffee after class to visit about volunteer opportunities	Sept 15, 20___	Accept volunteer opportunity
3. Lisa Drouin	Current Donor $2,500	Tom Button	Doug McMillan	College Preparatory Programming	$15,000	B	Tom call and personally invites to tour college prep classroom	Oct 15, 20___	Agrees to come on college preparatory classroom tour

Propect Readiness Ranking: A: Ready to be solicited. B: Has interest, needs further cultivation; C: Need to qualify.

store. It can also be at a lunch meeting or a meeting especially designed for educating volunteers. It is a personal note written on an annual support campaign newsletter. It is a handwritten note or a quick e-mail to say "I thought of you today." The connection might be in sharing a small victory related to one of the challenges faced by your organization that you think they would enjoy hearing about. Be creative and make a point of connecting with your donors and prospects as often as is reasonable.

Some cultivation ideas for your consideration:

- Invitations to events that may be of interest, importance, or meaning to them
- Invitations to participate in non-fundraising activities
- Invitations to dine (lunch, breakfast, dinner) with people important to the cause
- Invitations to participate in insiders' groups
- Feature stories on the family, if appropriate and approved, in your newsletter
- Calls on their anniversary, birthday, graduation, and so on.
- Informal birthday greeting or other cards
- Thank-you gifts
- Thank-you notes
- Informal handwritten notes
- Newspaper clippings of interest ("I saw this and thought that you might be interested . . . ")
- Recognition of all kinds (banners, boards, newsletters, and so on.)
- Committee work
- Board service
- Individual celebratory events
- Other?

These ideas can and should be as diverse as the people you are cultivating; personal and heartfelt are two keys to success here!

Asking for the Gift

Now that you have realized the importance of developing relationships and have learned some key steps as to how and when to do it, we can look at the task of actually asking for a gift from someone. Whether you are recruiting someone as a volunteer or just asking someone to support your cause, at some point, you have to ask for the gift.

We have touched on asking for the gift a couple of times in this text, as it related to asking volunteers for money as they were being recruited and also in our telephone and email efforts. This is such an important topic in the annual support campaign that it is worthy of its own section here. Chapter 5 which focuses on recruiting volunteers, plus this chapter, will give you the information that you need to really move your annual campaign forward. We must be willing to ask, help others to ask, encourage others to ask, and teach others to ask, if we are to have successful annual support campaigns. There are some great books whose topics focus only on making the ask, and I certainly recommend that you learn from those as well.

My goal here is to give you the skills and tips that you need to go forth and make some good solicitations. While you may not be the most seasoned or expert solicitor after reading this section, you will have the tools you need to begin your campaign success. I have been on some pretty poorly done solicitation calls that just because the ask was made, money was given. Remember, if you do not ask, you will more than likely not get.

Asks Bring More than Just Money

While raising charitable dollars is usually the motivating factor, asking for a charitable gift has a number of other benefits. One very significant benefit is the chance to tell the story of your organization in the community. The opportunity to get the message out about the tremendous work your organization is doing is of real value. While the ask is about giving people an occasion to give, it is also a public relations opportunity and a way to continue to learn about the person, corporation, foundation, or other entity that you are asking for charitable funds. This is a perfect arena to connect individuals or groups to your organization because you shared with them and they shared with you. The rewards are often monetary and more!

Another positive by-product of making an annual campaign ask is that it is cultivation at the same time it is actual fundraising. By this I mean that while you are asking for money for your annual support campaign, you are actually also laying the groundwork for future asks related to other gifts, whether annual, capital, or endowment in nature. Undoubtedly, asking for money is a key component of the annual support campaign and by doing so, you are also cultivating donors for the future. Good financial development programs build on themselves, and the annual support campaign can be a strong basis for your efforts in so many ways.

Another benefit of the annual campaign solicitation is simply the chance to practice asking for the gift. If you think of the annual support campaign as a continual learning arena, it liberates us to just ask. I often tell my clients that the annual support campaign is the time where we want to hear people say no if they are going to say it at all. Would you rather have someone say no to a $5,000 gift or a $500,000 gift? Usually we are making asks for smaller gifts during the annual support campaign, so it is a time to learn and grow for both the donor and the organization.

The annual campaign ask is also an excellent time to learn about how people feel and think about your organization. A typical donor dialogue might go something like this:

A: Do you love our nonprofit organization?

B: Yes.

A: Do you love our programs?

B: Yes.

A: Do you love the mission work that we do?

B: Yes.

A: Will you make a charitable gift of $X to our organization?

B: You know, I would, but I really am not comfortable with _____ .

People will tell you how much they like and appreciate you until you ask them for money . . . then they will tell you what they really think! It is important to learn this information every year so that you can change that which needs changing and learn what is not worth changing! You do not want your donors to run the organization, but understanding what is and is not important to them sometimes can make the difference between surviving and thriving or living and dying as an organization.

Remember also that one goal of the annual support campaign is to utilize volunteers to ask the most probable and best gift-giving prospects. Utilize volunteers (and staff as appropriate) to make as many personal solicitations as possible. This should yield the most charitable dollars for your organization. As we discussed earlier in this book, we should make our best asks as personal and as well prepared as possible. When it comes to asking for the gift, a few key questions will help us determine how and when to make the solicitation call.

- Who is the best person(s) to solicit this gift?
- Are these prospects ready (or ready enough) to give?
- Do you need or have more time to cultivate their interest?
- How much could they give if properly motivated?
- What would motivate them to give more?
- Is there something in your case that might be especially appealing to them?
- Who is the best team to cultivate and solicit the prospect: staff/volunteer or volunteer/volunteer?

 TIPS AND TECHNIQUES

A few foundational concepts to remember before asking:

- *People give to people with good causes.* Your volunteers and staff members need to be the people donors give to, and your cause needs to be one of integrity and positive movement in the community. Not all nonprofits have good causes. If you work for one of these, change jobs or re-engineer, revamp, or retool the cause!

(continued)

- *Make your own gift first.* Before we ask others to give, we ourselves must first give. Unless we do this before we go out into the community to ask, we greatly jeopardize our chance for success as well as our own credibility. An "asker" is far more convincing when they have dug into their own wallets, and have made a financial gift themselves first.

- *Seek pledges for larger gifts.* Pledging gives people the ability to make their payments over time and budget it into their monthly and annual expenses. Especially for individuals who are making their gift out of their annual income, pledging can help make for larger gifts.

- *Be persistent.* Note that I do not say be annoying or overwhelming. Be professionally persistent without alienating donors or prospects in any way. Remember that annual campaigns are done every year so you will be back again to ask for another gift before you know it. *Never* make an enemy, but do be polite and persistent in your quest for the gift. After all, it is for a great cause!

Tips on Getting a Meeting to Make the Ask

- Know that when you get an opportunity to see someone, your chances for getting a gift go *way* up!

- Sending a letter in advance of calling for an appointment can boost your confidence. A letter from a volunteer is most effective (ideally on the person's own stationery; it is more personal).

- Practice what you are going to say on the telephone before you pick it up.

- Have a script ready but speak freely.

- Have your calendar handy and ready.

- Stand up and smile when you talk.

- Keep small talk brief. Move quickly to "coming to see them." Ask: "When is the best time to come see you? How is Tuesday at 2:00 or Thursday at 9:00 in the morning?"

- Be up front about the time you will need but get what you can.

- Be focused and *be prepared to listen.*

- Move the conversation and set a date.
- You got an appointment!

Listen!

Ask is usually thought of as a verb about talking, but ironically, in fundraising, "the ask" is also very much about listening too. Everyone is eager to tell about their case for giving, their nonprofit organization, and their plans for the future, but a large component of the ask is about listening. Listening is a skill that all too many of us have lost or never honed. It involves not only hearing but also taking in the information and making it part of the learning process. *Really* listen to your donors and prospects, and you will have much more success in getting and keeping charitable gifts. People who listen well make much better fundraisers because they can meet donors where they are rather than dragging donors somewhere they do not want to go. Our goal as solicitors is to hear the passions that resonate with donors and to make those passions become reality through our nonprofit work. If we hear what donors are looking for, we can do a better job of connecting them at the right place to our organization. By actively listening, we help to ensure that we will make the best solicitation possible. More than any other step, listening is a vital part of the solicitation process. Try not to overhear the nos; hear instead what excites them about the work that you are doing.

Making the Ask

For many years, I have used a ten-step approach to teach and explain the annual support campaign solicitation process. By breaking the process down into simple steps, conversations and solicitations seem to be well planned and also to progress well. Dividing the solicitation call into multiple steps enables us to make sure that we are keeping on track in our conversation and also lets us share the work when we are working as part of a solicitation team. Don't forget to listen more than you talk!

Ten Steps to an Annual Support Campaign Ask

1. Introduce yourself and the purpose of your visit. Talk about why you are there and who you are if the prospect does not know you well. State that you are a volunteer and/or staff person doing this out of your personal belief in the nonprofit organization and your strong conviction about its importance to the community. Share your feelings and tell your story of why the organization is so important to you. Listen to and watch how the donor responds.

2. Ask questions that establish the prospect's understanding of the nonprofit organization that you are representing. Example: What has been your experience with the organization? Do you and your children or friends use and enjoy or benefit from the mission personally? What do you think are the important roles that this organization serves in our community? Do you know others who have benefited from the organization specifically? *Listen and hear!*

3. Share your personal convictions about the nonprofit and its importance in the community. Make it a two-way conversation by asking questions, then pausing so that the prospect can contribute too. Idea: Tell why you think the nonprofit is important and share what your involvement has been. Building on step 1, rather than speaking about yourself personally, here your focus is on the organization. *Watch body language, listen and hear!*

4. State this year's case for giving and the important work that it will accomplish. Do this after you have heard about the prospect's interests and passions, and do your best to align this year's case with those passions without misrepresenting the work that you are trying to do. Explain how your community will be better because of this valuable community asset. *Watch body language, listen and hear!*

5. Ask about the prospect's area of interest. What part of this project does the person feel most strongly about, and why? What about the annual support campaign case is most interesting to the prospect? What about it may be

interesting to other family members? Remember to listen. This is where you can make the lines of connection to your organization that can strengthen over time and really help you get the gift. *Watch body language, listen and hear!*

6. Ask for the gift. Ask for a specific amount. "We were hoping that you would consider making a gift in the range of $500 per month. Could you do that to help ___ in our community?" This type of statement allows the donor to know what you are hoping for and expecting from him or her in terms of making a gift. Without a specific ask amount, the donor has no idea what your hopes and aspirations are for this part of the fundraising effort. Remember to use information from the prospect's area of interest to ask for a specific amount, then *wait for the prospect to respond* without talking further. After you have asked . . . *wait*. Give the prospect time to *think* and respond before you speak. The prospect is processing the information, and this processing takes a minute. It may be a hard few seconds for the asker at first, but the prospect is busy thinking. Think positively—they may not be contemplating whether or not to give you the money, they may be deciding which account to give it to you out of, or even if they want to give you more than you asked for!

There is an old adage in fundraising that is not totally true that says, "Whoever speaks first after the ask is made loses." If you are newer to fundraising, take this comment to heart. If you are more experienced, make sure that you are mostly following this practice in your solicitations. Remember not to apologize for asking for the funds. It is a good cause and these funds are needed and important! *Watch body language, listen and hear!*

7. Take out the pledge card only after the person says yes. Paperwork is merely a distraction and is irrelevant before you get a positive response. Once the prospect says yes, you can anchor the thought and arrangement with a written pledge card. If you do not get a yes, do not take out the card.

8. Ask about matching gifts. Again, do so only after prospects say yes. Some companies do match gifts; if your donor works for such an organization, you can grow your gift with some simple additional paperwork.

9. Fill out the pledge card with the donor and get a signature. Fill out the card as completely as possible so that the nonprofit office has current and accurate information. Feel free to write additional information on the pledge card as needed and appropriate.

10. Thank the donor for his or her generosity. You have done it! Thank the person at the time, then immediately send out a personal, handwritten thank-you note as well. Transmit the gift information to the nonprofit office as soon as possible so that it can be processed and in the system and goal calculations.

TIPS AND TECHNIQUES

Things to Remember about Asking

- Anticipate your prospect's questions when possible and have answers ready whenever you can.
- Re-review the solicitation plan materials just before the meeting with the prospect.
- Ask for a specific dollar amount: "We were hoping that you would consider making a gift in the range of $500 per month. Could you do that to help ___ in our community?"
- Once you have asked, give your donor/prospect ample time to think and respond—*wait*.

Something you might be thinking now is "What if the prospect says no?" Well, that does happen sometimes even with the best-laid plans. Remember that philanthropy is often defined as "joyful giving"; perhaps the person is not ready to joyfully give . . . just yet.

What do you do? Well, it depends on just how hard a no it really is. Sometimes a no is just a response that people really need more information or time to be comfortable making a gift. What is keeping them from making the gift? Try to dig, respectfully and carefully, to find out what the issues are or lack of interest is. Again, and always, remember to try to find out the information without being annoying. Every meeting with a donor or prospect is also cultivation for every future meeting. How you handle this no may determine how next year's meeting goes.

Asking for a gift is part art and part science, and when you receive a no from a prospective donor, it is a particularly artful time You want to overcome every objection that you can while remaining true to the donor and the organization. Askers often walk this balancing act as they strive to serve the interests of both the donor and the organization. Remember it is a great time to learn about the prospect, what their capacity is, what their commitment is, and so on. Some prospects have very good reasons why they do not want to give a gift; we need to honor and respect those feelings and motives. Some donors will not give to you this year, and their reasons may be valid. Honor them with dignity and thank them for their time. Yet there may be no good reason at all why they are not giving. Such casual objections are the ones you want to counter.

 IN THE REAL WORLD

I was once making an informational request from a foundation for an organization that I was serving. When I asked if it would ever support an organization like the one I was representing, the person on the telephone (the foundation head) stated that the foundation's mission was to fund organizations in a different city from where mine was. When I asked this follow-up question, "So there is never a reason that you might fund an organization like mine?" the foundation head stated, "Most people don't make it this far. Since you asked, there was a time actually last year where we did fund an organization similar to yours." I thanked him for his time and made arrangements to connect with this foundation over the course of the next 12 months. Within a year, this foundation was a major donor to our nonprofit organization. If I had listened to the first seeming no and not pursued the relationship, we would never have engaged this foundation in the important work that we were doing in that community.

- Use closed end suggestion/questions to request specific dollar amounts. For example: "We are here today to ask you for a gift of $25,000 for our annual campaign to send children with severe medical needs to camp. Would you do that for these kids?"
- Remember that objections and questions are often ways of asking for more information.
- Get pledge commitments in writing.
- Be prepared if the opportunity presents itself to discuss deferred and planned giving.
- Remember that no does not mean never, it just means "not now."
- *Always* conclude *every* presentation with a "thank you."
- If another appointment is necessary, schedule it at the end of the meeting itself so that you can follow-up and involve all appropriate parties easily.

Follow Up after the Visit

What you do after the meeting should not be left up to chance. Remember that every meeting—even the ones where you actually are asking for money—is a cultivation and preparation for the next meeting and the next gift. You want to take every opportunity to bring the donor/prospect closer to your organization, and immediately after any meeting is a great time to do this step. I find that when I do these things immediately after the meeting, I do not forget to do them. By taking a few moments to debrief right after a meeting, you keep the facts straight and next steps are often easy to make happen. Here are a few steps to think about as soon as you leave an appointment, whether it went great or not so well.

Debrief the Asking Team Immediately

Meet with everyone involved in the meeting itself (except the donor/prospect) and talk about the call and how it went. It does not have to be long to be effective. It can even be done in the car ride back to the office. What went well? What went less well? What did we learn? What facts about the donor and prospect did we learn? So many pieces of information will be fresh in your mind—write them down now! They are invaluable pieces of the relationship puzzle.

Plan the Next Steps for the Donor/Prospect

Right after you leave the donor/prospect, you and the other person who went on the call with you should arrange the next steps and decide who can do them with relative ease. Write down who will do each of the next steps, and follow up with an email as a confirmation and reminder for both of you. Some things you might discuss include:

- Who will write follow-up thank-you notes for the meeting/gift? (Both of you!?)

- How should we announce the gift, if appropriate (newsletter, recognition listings, newspaper, etc.)? Make sure that you have the donor's permission before going public.

- How will follow-up steps such as administrative thank-you letters be handled? Optimally, a system is in place so that when the staff or a volunteer gets a gift or pledge, certain things happen automatically: thank-you letters, data entry, invoicing, billing, appropriate donor recognition, and so on.

- Do we need to set a follow-up meeting if we did not get the gift on this call?

- What are the next steps in engaging the donor further if appropriate? (Such steps might include setting up a program visit, meeting with a key person or volunteer at the agency, getting the spouse more involved in the organization, etc.)

- Whom should we talk to at our nonprofit to help the donor take the next step (the financial department, the CEO, the program area, etc.)?

- Other?

The fact is that now is the time—right after the call has occurred—to think about and implement your next steps; information is fresh and key people are together. Do it now, and you will have fewer mistakes in follow-up and better information to work with moving forward.

Donor and Volunteer Acknowledgments

All too often in our nonprofit organizations and in our profession as fundraisers, we get a gift and do not do enough to thank our donors for their generosity. Think about what someone does when they make even the smallest of contributions to our nonprofits. They are giving a valuable limited resource to our organizational cause. They are giving their trust to us. They are saying to us that they value us enough to give us money to further the tremendous work that we are doing. They are stating that they are willing to become associated with us as a donor. This and so much more goes with making a charitable gift.

When you really look at all that goes into making a charitable gift, nonprofit organizations should be thanking and valuing their donors abundantly from the very beginning of their relationship, regardless of the size of the gift or the prestige of the donor.

But we are not.

Often donors and prospects feel that the only time we contact them is to ask for money. With the often-constant need for funds and the inevitability of more and greater needs that so many nonprofits deal with daily, it is easy to understand why nonprofits do not thank more and why donors feel as they do.

But it is not acceptable.

I challenge you to look—right now—at all of the programs that your organization does, no matter how large or small your nonprofit. Look at all of the things that you do and find me one—just one program—that has a higher profit margin than philanthropy. Odds are that you will not find one. Yet rather than investing in this golden goose in our organizations, by thanking and valuing our donors, all too often we go on after receiving a gift as if we are totally entitled to have received the benefit.

In the donor–nonprofit world, nonprofit organizations need to do a much better job of saying thank you. We ask for gifts regularly, but more often than not we do a poor job of showing thanks and appreciation to our donors. We are often on to the next gift. We are almost always better served to thank and appreciate our existing donors than to ignore this step and instead spend our time finding new ones.

Do not let this be the situation at your nonprofit. Value your donors in the way that they deserve. This does not mean lavishing them with overpriced gifts or inappropriate trinkets. Instead, it means showing true appreciation by reporting back to them how their gift was used and being as sincere and personal as possible in thanking them. A foundation board member recently told me that they had hundreds of plaques in a closet at their foundation. Plaques, they told me, were never what they wanted. Make your appreciation something that really speaks to the donor. Be creative! Donors really do not want you to spend the money that they just gave you to buy them something that will end up in a closet or worse. Again, the thank-you does not have to be expensive, just thoughtful.

Here are some things that may help your donor appreciation program:

- Understand donor recognition and retention. New and longtime donors should be especially valued.

- Remember to recognize your volunteers who help you get the gift and/or make the ask. Reward them by thanking them.

- Create and manage a system that thanks donors *multiple* times each year. When people give you a gift that affects lives through an entire year, let them know how that gift is being put to work all year long. For example, share with the donor how the children in the program in the economically challenged neighborhood are doing better in school this year because of the tutoring, new technology, and improved after-school programs that they funded.

- Use pledge collections and donor retention tools to communicate thanks. Write something special about the donor's gift on the bottom of pledge

TIPS AND TECHNIQUES

Donor Thanks

- Personalize—write a personal thank you.
- Send within 48 hours.
- Explain how funds will be used.
- Utilize thank-you calling banks.
- Have staff and/or volunteers call a few donors every day.
- Understand that recognizing and thanking is the first step to the next gift . . . create meaningful ways to accomplish this. For example, if your nonprofit does animal rehabilitation, consider sending photos of newly rehabilitated animals in communications with past donors.
- Consider public recognition (if appropriate), especially for corporate gifts where money given may be from marketing budget dollars.
- Send a personalized organizational thank-you letter. You have already sent a personal thank-you after your visit; this letter states that the gift was received, processed, and how much it means to the organization.
- Arrange a follow-up phone call from a key person (board chair or member, chief executive officer, etc.) in the organization as soon as possible after the gift is made.

statements/bills/invoices. Use extra space on different documents to maximize how much you appreciate and value donors.

- Honor government requirements for acknowledgments. Check with the appropriate governmental agency in your country to make sure that you are doing what is required.
- Remember that a thank–you is likely required to
  - Increase the donor's next gift.
  - Secure future gifts.

Summary

Cultivating donors and asking for money are two key steps in any strong annual support campaign program. Without strong relationships, asking for funds will be less comfortable and also less successful. Relationships are the basis of solid nonprofit work and volunteer and prospect engagement. With more people involved and engaged in the work that we do, we will raise more money and ultimately accomplish more of our charitable mission work. Implementing the Donor Cultivation Process at your nonprofit will help to divide and categorize your donor pool which will help organize and focus your efforts.

Asking for money is the most effective way of raising it for our organizations. While this may seem obvious, many of our nonprofits wait for people to drop money on their doorsteps. By building the relationship first and then asking for charitable support, you have the best formula for making the gift happen. By asking for money in the most personal way practical and possible, we increase the chances to raise the most money possible, from our constituency and our public.

Most of us do not thank our donors nearly enough or show them the appreciation they deserve. By appropriately showing appreciation to our donors, we let them know that they are highly valued, and we also help to ensure our next gift is a meaningful contribution from them. Honoring and appreciating donors is not only a valuable part of any good annual support campaign program; it is also critical foundational work for future gifts. Thanking and reporting back to donors may be some of the best investments in our organizational futures that we can make.

Build relationships, ask for money, and then thank, report back to, and value your donors.

## CHAPTER 8

Planning and Evaluating Your Campaign

After reading this chapter, you will be able to:

- Create and institute an annual support campaign plan based on defined goals and objectives.
- Assess where your organization currently is regarding the annual support campaign.
- Set a monetary goal for your annual support campaign.
- Evaluate your campaign and recognize the value in doing so.

Planning for a well-run and highly effective annual support campaign is much like planning any other effort that you might do in your life or work. The more that you can see and understand the landscape ahead of you, the more prepared you will be for whatever arises during your efforts. Just as with any endeavor, it is important for you to think about what results you want to get before you do the campaign. Having a clear plan for what you want to achieve will allow you to formulate a clear path for obtaining your annual campaign goals and objectives.

Included in this chapter is a timeline to help you plan the months of your annual support campaign as well as sections on the events, overall spirit of the campaign, and goal setting. Last, we cover evaluation and how valuable an exercise this review can be for learning from this campaign and planning for the next.

What Are Your Objectives?

If you asked the chief executive officer (CEO), the board chair, the board of directors, and high-ranking staff to state what the annual support campaign optimally should achieve for your organization, you could get a handful of different answers. For some, the annual support campaign's objective would be to gain a larger base of donors or an increase in the number of volunteers. For others, it would be to get your organizational mission information out into the community more or to increase the general community awareness of your organization. The CEO may want the board of directors or the staff to be more involved. Of course, for many, the number-one reason to do the annual support campaign would be to raise charitable support dollars. Everyone would be right, and there are certainly more answers than these. To have a clear direction and for all to feel successful in the end, you must decide what your main objectives for this annual support campaign will be. If each faction is trying to address its own independent perceived goal without consideration of the others, your campaign will have less focus and likely not achieve any of the goals as well as possible.

Exercise

Take a moment now and think about what is important to you and to the culture at your nonprofit organization.

What are the top two things you want to achieve in your annual support campaign? List those things here:

1.

2.

What are the top two things you think that your supervisor wants to achieve in the annual support campaign? List those things here:

   1.
   2.

What things do you believe will be important to the chair of your board of directors? List those things here:

   1.
   2.

If you were to ask your largest donors what would be important about your upcoming annual campaign, what would they say are the two most important things? List those things here:

   1.
   2.

Are there any other individuals or entities (such as your overall board of directors) whose concerns might be important to understand? List those here:

   1.
   2.

Ideally, you would have several conversations with key individuals and stakeholders in your organization about the annual support campaign and what each wants to accomplish with its implementation. Each constituency may see the annual support campaign as filling a different purpose or need in your organization. Understanding the motivations and desires of each person may be important not only to your own job evaluation but also to the organization's view of campaign success. Additionally, knowing what expectations each group might have, will help you realize what is important to each and will allow you to construct a more unified, final group of objectives. If you can, take the time to fully understand the goals and objectives for your management and leadership regarding annual support. It will be time well spent in the short and the long run.

Deciding When to Do Your Campaign

As stated in Chapter 3, the best time to have a fundraising campaign is likely when you and your organization are ready to do so. Carefully considering your organizational calendar is also a good first step.

Looking at several key questions will help you to determine when the right time is for you and your nonprofit to have an annual campaign:

- What times of year are staff particularly stretched from other demands on their time?

- When are volunteers more or less available to do this type of work?

- What other fundraising efforts are going on in your community and at what time?

- How can you organize volunteers to work on these efforts without the distractions of major holidays or other key events that would take their focus away from the work at hand?

- What budgetary pressures are part of your organizational reality that need to be considered in making this decision?

- When is a 4–8 week period of time that makes sense to run the public aspect of this campaign given the above questions? The 12 month campaign timeline is a helpful tool as you begin to outline your plan for an annual campaign.

By determining when the best time to have a campaign is for your organization, you can utilize the timeline in the next section to help make sure that you do the necessary work to make it successful. Campaigns need time to develop—especially on the volunteer side of things—if they are to be successful. Volunteer recruitment and engagement takes time and if you short cut that part of this process, you will be hard pressed to achieve all that you can. Plan for your next annual campaign with enough lead time and you give yourself and your organization a real chance at greatness. Plan for your annual campaign hastily and you will more likely fail or be doomed to underachieve.

Creating Your Annual Campaign Plan

One item that helped me when I was doing annual support campaigns year in and year out, as a direct hands-on leader and campaign director, was to have a timeline for what needed to occur when. I created these timelines by using them over a period of years and adding to them yearly. These timelines might not be perfect, but they will get you off to a great start in managing your own annual support campaign at your nonprofit. Rework and hone your plan each year, so that it becomes a solid working document for you.

Sample 12-Month Annual Campaign Timeline

9 Months Prior to Public Campaign Start

❒ Run list of all of last year's campaign volunteers and how much they raised. This list should contain name, address, phone numbers, and amount raised.

❒ Secure overall annual campaign chair.

❒ Meet with staff and key volunteers to finalize and discuss potential volunteer leadership ideas for campaign.

❒ Major gift donor cultivation strategies are developed and reviewed and implementation is begun.

❒ Develop goals for recruiting volunteers with senior staff and campaign chair.

❒ What will our campaign goal be for number of volunteers involved this year giving one gift and getting at least one other? What will be the monetary goal associated with the campaign? How many in our community will we try to help with the money raised?

8 Months–7 Months Prior to Public Campaign Start

❒ Mail notes from staff and key volunteers thanking last year's volunteers for helping. In thank you note, discuss if you can how the money is already having a positive impact.

❑ Plan thank-you-thons for one to two months from now.

❑ Meet with last year's Campaign Executive Committee and this year's campaign chair to review the evaluations and statistics from last year's campaign and make recommendations to next year's committee

❑ Appoint new campaign executive committee. This is usually made up of Annual Campaign Chair, Campaign Director (staff), Major Gifts Chair, Community Gifts Chair, Board Solicitation Chair, and Staff Campaign Chair as appropriate.

❑ Continue implementation of individual major gift cultivation strategies.

❑ Senior staff/volunteers call major gift donors who did and did not give per report from last month.

❑ Review budget for this year: Is it realistic? Alter for this year as appropriate.

❑ Build the case statement for this year's campaign.

❑ Form spirit committee for upcoming campaign efforts. This is the group of people that is usually made up of a combination of staff and volunteers who help to make the campaign meetings happen in a fun and exciting way. Organizing everything from decorations to food, they make the campaign meetings feel like special events to add a fun flair to the campaign effort as appropriate to your organizational culture. (Do not forget to involve volunteers here as well.) Who are the people who can add great spirit and energy to our efforts this year?

❑ Develop staff job descriptions for this year; review last year's.

❑ Meet with staff to discuss collection strategies for this year and how process went last year.

❑ Select and solidify campaign theme. *Name* the campaign. Spirit Committee should be involved in naming. (One of my favorite campaign themes was, "People are the Heart of the Matter" which was done by a human services agency that I worked with earlier in my career. Staff and volunteers dressed up as medical professionals and campaign meetings had a fun spirit with medical jokes, witty skits and clever decorations.)

☐ Begin planning for major donor event that is three months away. This is the event where major donors from the last campaign are both honored and thanked as appropriate.

6 Months Prior to Public Campaign Start

☐ Mail volunteer T-shirts to all who volunteered on last year's campaign with a letter saying something like "As the weather gets warmer, we wanted to thank you again." The important note here is that you think of a fun way to thank your volunteers throughout the year.

☐ Review campaign job descriptions for accuracy and organization. Restock the administrative file drawers of all printed materials as appropriate so they can be used and mailed quickly and as needed.

☐ Campaign executive committee meets to review draft of the annual support campaign plan, which includes:

Case for giving

Upcoming campaign calendar

Campaign organization chart

Campaign expense budget

Overall campaign success indicators/benchmarks/goals

> Once these documents have been finalized, add them to your administrative files as well. You will want to be able to mail out the case, calendar and even the organizational chart as appropriate to volunteers as they are recruited to your overall campaign.

☐ Secure major gifts chair.
☐ Secure community gifts chair.
☐ Continue implementing individual major gifts cultivation strategies.
☐ Continue major gifts list building for potential campaigners and contributors.

❏ Secure board solicitation committee chair.

❏ Secure staff solicitation chair.

❏ Finish recruiting any leadership vacancies absolutely no later than this month. This includes getting remainder of Campaign leadership in place: chair, major gifts chair, community gifts chair, staff solicitation chair.

❏ Plan and organize campaign calendar: *finalize* all dates for upcoming campaign.

❏ Senior staff report details/reasons for nongiving from major donors.

❏ Hold thank-you-thon this month. This is where donors are contacted by phone or other appropriate communication and thanked for their gift from last year. Ideally, donor thanks happens in a timely manner when the gift is actually given. This contact makes sure that the donor is kept connected with the organization about how their gift is being used and how much they are truly appreciated for making their gift.

❏ Pledge collection follow up: Where are we with collections and what is our plan to raise percentages?

❏ Continue planning for major donor event that is two months away.

❏ Write newsletter to donors and volunteers from last year's campaign letting them know how the money was allocated and how it is being used to positively better your community.

5 Months Prior to Public Campaign Start

❏ Coordinate calendar with appropriate entities (caterer, conference rooms, hotels, etc.) by month-end.

❏ Send newsletter out alerting all donors of how their money is being spent. (Include a way for donors to communicate with the nonprofit if they are willing to help again this year: a return postcard, email address, or other response medium.

❏ Meet with major gifts chair, community gifts chair and any other volunteer leaders to select names of prospective team leaders and members.

❏ Finish planning for major gifts donor event next month.

❏ Continue implementing all donor cultivation strategies.

❏ Complete staff solicitation plan.

❏ Recruit staff solicitation team.

❏ Make final push with this season's (spring, summer, fall, etc.) recruiting to get as many new and old volunteers involved with the upcoming campaign.

❏ Meet with staff to generate new campaign prospects for donors and as further volunteer support for teams.

4 Months Prior to Public Campaign Start

❏ Follow up with campaign collections from last year. Where are we with collections, and what is our plan to increase percentages of collections?

❏ Hold major gifts donor event thanking last year's donors.

❏ Meet with all staff members to make sure they fully understand their campaign assignments.

❏ Put campaign marketing plan in place if you have not already done so. (internal and external).

❏ Continue to secure all volunteer team members.

❏ Continue implementing individual donor cultivation strategies.

❏ Begin to finalize all volunteer fundraising teams from a recruitment perspective. What teams need more people to be successful? How can we help those volunteer leaders to get more volunteers involved on their campaign teams? Who are prospects that we can connect to the teams who need the most support at this point?

❏ Confirm matching gift information for upcoming phon-a-thon.

3 Months Prior to Public Campaign Start

❏ Recruit and have in place all team leaders and team members by first of next month.

❏ Have staff campaign cultivation/motivational event (to build enthusiasm and motivation prior to working closely with campaign volunteers and being asked for their gift).

❏ Order and have in place volunteer thank you gifts for upcoming campaign.

❏ Write second newsletter on how last year's annual campaign money is being spent. Focus on the positive impact that it is having and remember to deal with issues of both the head and the heart!

❏ Send out invitations to any upcoming meeting three weeks before meeting date. (see public campaign calendar)

❏ Get pictures for any gift or video usage in this year's campaign. (These pictures refer to photos or artwork that you might use in anything ranging from a promotional video to a thank you photo for donors or volunteers.)

❏ Assign prospects to staff solicitation committee members.

❏ Hold staff solicitation coaching session.

❏ Have staff solicitation committee complete visits this month.

❏ Meet with Campaign executive committee to check and discuss campaign progress.

❏ Work through process for clearing all donor prospects prior to distribution with or to volunteers. (This process involves making sure that the right prospects get to the right volunteers. It also makes it so that if two different volunteers want the same person to ask, the decision is made as to who gets that person.)

❏ Secure community gifts members as needed.

❏ Develop plan for meeting/event participation by volunteers.

2 Months Prior to Public Campaign Start

❏ Send out second newsletter containing information on how money is being spent.

❏ Continue to manage RSVPs for upcoming meetings.

❏ Finalize board solicitation committee as needed. Recruit any needed individuals who are not already recruited.

❐ Prepare for board solicitation committee meeting where board members determine how much to ask all individual board members to give this year.

❐ Prepare name tags, calendars, job descriptions, pledge cards, case statements, volunteer information cards, organizational charts for all levels, team lists as they stand today with full information including name, address, phone numbers, email, position, level, prospect lists, and so on. Prepare all of this for the upcoming meetings with volunteer teams.

❐ Order meals for meetings as appropriate.

❐ Confirm upcoming meeting locations.

❐ Produce all campaign materials in final form.

❐ Order all campaign incentive items. These are fun items or prizes that are given out as reward for positive volunteer participation. For example, most gifts to the campaign, largest gift, most asks, most volunteers recruited, etc.

❐ Community gifts chair and team leaders meet to select prospects for continued volunteer recruitment.

❐ Recruit all community gifts team leaders.

❐ Photographer: Set up dates as appropriate for upcoming events/meetings.

❐ Set participant/beneficiary testimonials for meetings.

❐ Hold campaign leadership meeting to include all chairs and team leaders as appropriate. Prepare these items for this meeting: Name tags, testimonials, list of all people who will be attending, list of people who worked in the campaign last year broken out for each team leader, and a list of any new people as possible volunteers broken out for each team leader (from last month's meeting). These names will be used to fill out last minute team recruitment efforts. There is still time to increase the volunteer strength of our teams—more volunteers makes for a stronger campaign! Also, prepare calendars, job descriptions, case, volunteer information cards, and team organizational charts for all leadership levels as appropriate.

❐ Plan agenda for upcoming meeting and confirm with all involved.

❐ Hold team leaders meeting.

❏ Get *all* team leaders pictures *this month* for use in promotional information as appropriate.

❏ Staff campaign this month and next: appropriate staff to attend all staff meetings to promote staff campaign.

❏ Complete staff campaign by middle of next month: promoted with a progress report no later than first of month with weekly reminders.

❏ Collection follow-up: Where are we with collections, and what is the plan to raise percentages? (This continues to be repeated because you want to collect or understand any outstanding debts from donors before going back to them again. Also you have already invested the time in getting the gift from them; make the most of that investment by collecting this pledge if possible.)

❏ Prepare for any audio, video, YouTube, etc, which must be done next month (if doing one).

1 Month Prior to Public Campaign Start

❏ Finalize location of all events and menus.

❏ Put final campaign office support systems in place. This includes the automatic things that should happen when they are triggered by a gift being received such as thank you notes, billing, etc.

❏ Begin board of directors solicitation.

❏ Hold campaign executive committee meeting to review progress to date and strategize as needed.

❏ Complete master list of prospective contributors.

❏ Continue implementing donor cultivation strategies.

❏ Major Gifts assignment meeting

❏ Clear prospects for community gifts team leaders.

❏ Finalize community gifts team campaigner recruitment.

❏ Finish recruiting and confirm information for all campaigners.

❐ Last chance for collection follow-up: next month closes books on last campaign year.

❐ Organize pledge cards and case statements.

❐ Review printed pledge cards for general accuracy and possible duplication errors. Pledge cards should be sorted to go to the correct teams and campaigners in major gifts and community gifts divisions. Remember that in a highly organized annual campaign, all potential donors names would be submitted to a central administrator for cross checking entries. The volunteers will receive pledge cards back with names of whom they should contact at the Campaign Kickoff. This pledge card system ensures that no one is asked multiple times and that the best person is making the ask.(Maybe someone knows your neighbor even better than you do!) This system is especially important for larger nonprofits and for the major gifts component of the campaign. If you do start your major gifts solicitation prior to the public phase, you will have to distribute their cards before the Kickoff event.

❐ Review system for distribution of pledge cards. What can we do to make this process run smoothly when we kickoff the public campaign?

❐ Complete audio, video, YouTube, etc to celebrate end of staff drive if appropriate.

❐ One week prior to first training: poster of thermometer in front of building, or some way to allow the community to stay current with campaign progress. It will be a way for some people to begin to be aware that there is a campaign going on.

❐ Three weeks prior to first training: banners up in building.

❐ One week prior to first training: pictures of all team leaders pictures posted in building.

❐ RSVPs for meeting. If you have not gotten RSVP's (that you have requested) for certain meetings, call to check the attendance status for that person. Make it a friendly call, it will no doubt serve as a reminder to them that the meeting is coming up!

❐ Order meals for meetings.

☐ Confirm upcoming meeting location.

☐ Photographer ready as appropriate.

☐ Testimonials of beneficiaries for meeting confirmed.

☐ Invitations sent out 3 weeks prior to each event.

☐ Plan all entertainment prior to events.

☐ Reporting boards: complete one week prior to kickoff. Reporting boards can be as simple as poster boards that announce the total money raised from the board and staff campaigns. (Note: at this point in the campaign, the private phase, which is the board and staff component, should be completed. By reporting the results, you give the next phase, which is the public community phase, information as well as momentum. Also, if you have given your major gifts component a "head start" to the public phase, you can report any gifts that they have brought in to date as well. This can bring a lot of energy to the group as they realize how much they already have raised towards your overall campaign goal.)

☐ Complete board of directors campaign.

☐ Senior staff and volunteers finish review of pledge cards for whom to ask and for how much, especially major gifts.

Public Campaign Starts!

Month 10: Public Campaign Month 1!

☐ Week of first training: facility totally decorated with theme to raise awareness and campaign anticipation.

Week 1

☐ Hold major gifts solicitation coaching session.
☐ Hold major gifts committee kickoff meeting. Pass out major gift pledge cards here.
☐ Community gifts team campaigners submit their preferred donor prospect list to the central administrative personnel for clearance.

Week 2

❏ Continue major gifts solicitation.

❏ Clear and assign community gifts donor prospects for team campaigners.

❏ Hold coaching sessions for community gifts campaigners.

Week 3

❏ Continue major gifts solicitation.

❏ Hold community gifts teams makeup coaching session for any campaigners recruited at the last minute.

Week 4

❏ Hold large kickoff event (held with all campaign community gifts and major gifts teams in attendance). Give updates about staff and board campaign totals raised as well as major gifts total raised to date. These campaign totals show money already raised in pledges and give community gifts teams excitement about their ability to raise funds. Pass out all remaining pledge cards here that we want to contact through our volunteer campaign efforts this year.

❏ Continue major gifts solicitation.

❏ Collect all completed campaign pledge cards weekly.

Month 11: Public Campaign Month 2 (Final Month)!

❏ Finalize invitations for all meetings. Follow-up on unknown RSVPs for all meetings. This builds and strongly encourages attendance.

❏ Continue major gifts solicitation.

❏ Continue community gifts teams solicitation.

❏ Hold weekly report meetings: some virtual and at least one in person if at all possible, planned around a meal. Send "campaign report" each week to all volunteers stating how much each team raised so far and the total campaign amount reported. It will create enthusiasm, impetus to keep going and perhaps friendly competition, all for the betterment of your nonprofit mission!

❐ Collect all completed campaign pledge cards weekly.

❐ Hold outrageously fun Victory Celebration (with *everyone* together).

❐ Create name tags, and all related meeting event information for Victory Celebration.

❐ Finalize and total all pledges and gifts for announcement at the Victory Celebration.

❐ Wrap up telemarketing and all electronic efforts—complete before Victory Celebration.

❐ Confirm food and meals for final meeting.

❐ Confirm meeting location with operations director or site person.

❐ Hire or plan for photographer as needed.

❐ Have great testimonial for meeting where someone who is close to or affected by the impactful work that this campaign provides, shares their story in a meaningful way.

Month after Campaign Closes

❐ Update all gift recognition boards as appropriate in the nonprofit office, and so on. These may include donor recognition boards or plaques in the lobby, that highlight the major gifts of certain giving levels each year, and so on.

❐ Make sure that all thank-you letters have been sent out for all pledges and gifts received.

❐ Send volunteer appreciation gifts to those who did not get them at victory celebration.

❐ Declare final total and finalize all gift and pledge records

❐ Have volunteer solicitors provide feedback as to which donors have potential to move to a higher giving level next year and recommend year-long cultivation strategies for appropriate donors for next year's efforts.

❐ Send final "campaign report" to all volunteers stating how much each team raised and the total campaign amount reported. Get absolute final collection of all campaign pledge cards.

❏ Run major gifts report for last year and this year to make sure no one was missed. Make plan for getting any gifts missed with wrap up team or staff as appropriate.

❏ Begin list building for next year's campaign leadership after evaluation of performance in current campaign.

❏ Order volunteer T-shirts or other thank you gift for thank-yous to be mailed later.

❏ Compile and summarize campaign evaluation results.

❏ Complete campaign evaluation study.

❏ Wrap-up: data entry of all pledges to be completed no later than day 10 of this month

Two Months after Campaign Closes

❏ Hold brief meeting with staff to discuss campaign: what went well, what could be improved next year. Write down ideas as they may be valuable improvements for next year's campaign.

❏ Hold thank-you celebration for staff.

❏ Begin post-campaign cleanup efforts.

❏ Mail evaluations and volunteer thank-you notes to those who did not fill them out at the Victory Celebration.

❏ Review, evaluate, and follow-up on major gifts solicitation as needed.

❏ Follow-up on community gifts solicitation as needed.

❏ Send appropriate thank-you cards to all donors/workers.

❏ Finalize report with all appropriate breakouts (matching gifts, major gifts, community gifts, etc.) by month-end.

❏ Determine and strategize who will be next year's annual campaign chair and begin to recruit them if you have not already secured them for next year's campaign.

As you can see from the timeline, a lot of organization is involved in planning and implementing a high-functioning annual support campaign: events, meetings, organizational systems, thank-you notes, thank-you- thons, volunteer recruitment timetables, and so much more. I can promise you that even this timeline is not fully complete and that there are things that you will come up with to improve, add or delete to this detailed checklist. Still, it will hopefully give you a very useable outline to begin or enhance your efforts. As well, if this is your first campaign, do not be daunted by the complexity of the timeline. As stated, this timeline was created over years, and was used for some very large campaigns with lots of volunteers. Start with the basics for your first campaign, or if you are a small nonprofit organization. I did my first annual campaign with virtually no formal plan at all but having a plan is always much better than not having one. Refer to this timeline each year to build up your campaign to be as complete as possible.

Campaign Meetings

Essentially, all campaign meetings are designed to generate and encourage volunteer recruitment and engagement in the annual support campaign and its mission. This means that all campaign meetings are designed to help volunteers understand their roles and what it is exactly that you are trying to accomplish through the annual support campaign. Each meeting should have a tightly built agenda around division, team, or general volunteer recruitment. Testimonials of some sort from a beneficiary of the important mission work that you are doing are extremely powerful at these meetings. They serve to remind veteran volunteers and help new volunteers to fully understand why they are involved in this effort. Testimonials also help to build commitment, spirit and enthusiasm around the work that you do with the most essential volunteer team you may have at your organization.

Campaign meetings (or events, as they are sometimes called) are designed to bring together large groups of people to accomplish some only slightly different objectives. While meetings are more work oriented, events are designed to train, kick off, report, and celebrate. Campaign events should be structured to encourage enthusiasm, confidence, team spirit, and continued understanding of the objectives, tools and techniques needed to be successful. You want all of your events to be fun, educational, and keep the campaign moving forward. If you do this, volunteers will look forward to the campaign each year and give their precious time again. If you make meetings and events laborious or lackluster, you will not be as successful long term as you could be, and you may lose people over time.

Events and meetings should:

- Be centered around a meal whenever feasible.
- Have a testimonial talking about the vital work that you are doing.
- Have tight agendas designed by staff.
- Have tight agendas managed and led by your volunteer leadership.
- Have details and decorations managed by staff but supported by volunteers (with rare exceptions).
- Be focused.
- Be targeted in their message.

The events should always use volunteer and staff time wisely and manage resources prudently, so they should have a definite purpose. The main event types that are often had for the annual support campaign include:

- *Recruiting meeting.* Discuss who will be asked to volunteer and ensure that no one is overlooked or asked twice.
- *Trainings.* Orient and train volunteer teams.
- *Kickoff.* Begin your campaign with gusto! Make this meeting/event as powerful and fun as possible. You want people to look forward to this event as one of your most fun and exciting of the year.
- *Reporting meetings.* Update everyone on how much has been raised so far and keep the momentum and enthusiasm high.
- *Victory Celebration.* Celebrate the money that has been raised and how the world will be a better place because of your annual support campaign.

Make this event/meeting so fun and exciting that people will do every-thing possible to attend.

- Other meetings are held as necessary within teams or campaign compo-nents like major gifts or community gifts but these are determined an managed by the team leaders or division leaders themselves.

With well-run and organized meetings and events, your campaign will be more effective, your volunteers will feel better supported, and your organiza-tion will be viewed in even higher esteem by those who are involved. Take your meetings and events seriously, and they will pay great dividends to you this year and in coming years.

Spirit Factor

If you were a volunteer, would you want to participate in your annual support campaign? Often we overlook the "fun factor" of our efforts as we get caught up in the serious task that is the annual support campaign. It is important for our volunteer and donor retention efforts that we make our campaigns as re-warding and interesting as possible for our participants so that they will want to help us in the future. Hard work does not have to be tedious and a grind. By making campaign events, communications, contests, incentives, and the like fun, you help to make sure that your volunteers and donors will want to come back again and again. Be creative and let your imagination go; this can be some-thing your whole community looks forward to every year!

IN THE REAL WORLD

Many of the annual support campaigns that I have been involved with have had campaign themes in an effort to make the hard work that is fundraising more fun for everyone. Some of these annual support campaigns included hundreds of people on the local level. As expected, there were meetings or gatherings around training, victory celebration, report nights, and so on, but the themes made them anything but mundane.

One of the most memorable campaign theme experiences that I remember was in a small southern community that had its campaign kickoff within two weeks of the 9/11 tragedy in New York. Some volunteers felt that we should cancel our annual support campaign because of the tragedy, but we went on in spite of their concerns. (Note: *Never* cancel your annual support campaign!) We decided that the campaign theme should be "Heroes Make All the Difference." At each meeting, people were encouraged to dress up as their favorite heroes. People came as everything from firemen to baseball players, and the evenings were lively because people were able to dress up and celebrate the fact that heroes make the world a better place. At the victory celebration, we brought the theme together with the fact that our campaign volunteers were real heroes for helping us to do our important work in the community by raising funds. The message was very well received, and we surpassed our campaign goals during a challenging time of fundraising for a very small nonprofit.

Making efforts fun and exciting can make hard work easier and more rewarding. As you plan for your annual support campaign, think about how you can make it more enjoyable and interesting for your campaign volunteers and staff.

Spirit is something that is hard to measure but is easy to see when it is either present or lacking. Obviously, you want the campaign spirit of your staff and volunteers to be positive. Many components make up a campaign's spirit, but here are a few things to think about as you determine how your campaign is shaping up. As you think about campaign planning, consider how you might positively affect each of these key ideas.

- Has your board bought in to the idea?
- Are your key volunteers excited about the upcoming effort?
- Is your campaign chair fired up about the impact that this effort will have in the community?
- Is your CEO enthused and participating fully in the effort?
- Are your staff members passionate about the difference that they can make through their efforts in the annual support campaign?
- Does your campaign have some type of "fun factor" built in?

- Do your staff members feel that they are valued and important in the campaign process?

- Do your volunteers feel valued and important in the campaign process?

- Do your staff members feel successful or beaten down in the process?

- Do your volunteers feel successful or more like failures as they work to achieve their campaign goals?

- Other?

As you can see, there are many areas to create and expand the upbeat spirit in your annual support campaign efforts. While it is tough to measure campaign spirit after the campaign, you can definitely feel the difference when it is positive or negative while it is happening. Work hard to have an atmosphere that is uplifting, enthusiastic, and eager, and your campaign will be more enjoyable and more rewarding, and you will inevitably raise more funds for your organization.

Assessing Where Your Organization Is Currently

There are many things to consider in your planning as you move forward with your annual support campaign. It is imperative to consider what is central to your nonprofit based on your culture, your board, your volunteers, your staff, the fundraising environment in your community, and all of the other factors that make up your annual support campaign. Understanding the dynamics of each and working to make progress is what should be your main goal. I often tell my consulting clients that "You are where you are," and that our goal is to move forward. By focusing on improvement without worrying too much about perfection, we can advance our efforts a great deal. Look at where you are in each of the next areas and put focused effort on improving each area, as appropriate, for your organization.

Board of Directors

The board of directors is the governing and overseeing body of the nonprofit organization. It is best when they recognize that one of their many responsibilities is to provide leadership and ensure financial security for the nonprofit. One way to do this is to fundraise and assist with the essential work of financial development, but it is important to remember that this is a process.

Start where you are with the board you have, and look for successes early on in your efforts. The first year, try to get key individuals engaged and on board with your annual support campaign process. If it is the second, third or hundredth year for your annual support campaign, look at how you can improve individual areas of board participation and performance. I have been involved with literally hundreds of annual support campaigns, but I have never seen a perfect one. The trick is to improve constantly, and the board area is no different from any other. Work to build a stronger board effort this year, whether year 1 or year 100, and then look to grow it even stronger next year.

How Many Board Members Do You Have?

Some nonprofit organizations have many board members while others have only a few. Regardless of your situation, understand the team that you have and its influence on the fundraising effort that is the annual support campaign.

What is your nonprofit's total number of board members? (If you are a federated nonprofit agency or an organization that has multiple schools, branches, or units, look at each entity individually in this and other exercises.)

What Percentage of Your Board Members Give an Annual Gift?

While this may seem simple at first, it is important that your board members give to the annual support campaign for several reasons. Nonprofits often get board members to support different efforts, such as special events or other fundraising causes. Going forward, you should consider trying to get each board member to give to the annual support campaign. Some boards are engaged in things like the purchase of raffle or gala tickets and buying tables at events; these gifts do not represent a total and true philanthropic gift to the charitable organization. While raffle ticket or other type purchases may be given out of concern for the well-being of the nonprofit, it does not represent the truest form of philanthropy. Oftentimes, these other fundraising efforts are not even profitable or beneficial to the organization. An annual support campaign gift represents one of the most pure and consistent forms of philanthropy. It shows that your organization is important enough to be worthy of an annual support gift. It shows that the board member is truly committed to the cause that is your organization and the many programs and services that it offers. It also is likely the highest margin of return of philanthropic gifts to your organization. This usually makes the annual gift the most generous gift for a board member to give.

Another reason that it is important for board members to give annual gifts is that as your organization goes out into the corporate or foundation community, you will be asked, "How much did your board give, and what is their rate of participation?" Before you ask for large gifts from others, it is important that your board is actively connected and supportive in this important work. In addition, board members who can honestly say that they themselves have supported this effort with their gift, provides a most powerful message to prospective donors. In some situations, the subtle gauntlet of prestige and keeping up appearances will be at play.

Take the total number of board members making a gift and divide it by the number of total board members serving your organization. This will give you the percentage of board members making a charitable gift. What percentage of your board members gives an annual support campaign gift?

Board Members Helping to Raise Money

Board members have a fiduciary responsibility to help make sure that the nonprofit organization has the funds that it needs to fulfill its charitable mission. This is usually a very large task, as missions are often almost unachievable in totality and board members' abilities are limited by their time and other commitments. With all of this said, however, it is important that board members are willing to play an active role in charitable support. In an ideal world, board members are some of your biggest fans and strongest advocates. They know your organization better than almost anyone. Because of this, they often make the best storytellers about the worthy work that you are doing. Board members who use their abilities to tell the story of your organization in the community serve as soundly educated, capable, and passionate fundraisers. If board members do not embrace this admirable work, then your organization can still do an annual campaign, but it will never be as good as it can be. Remember that securing board involvement can take time and is a process. Whether your board is actively engaged now should not affect your decision to undertake an annual support campaign. As with any other annual support campaign issue related to readiness, you begin where you are and move forward.

Take the total number of board members who are actually helping you to raise annual support campaign funds and divide it by the number of total board members serving your organization. This will give you the percentage of board members who are helping you to raise annual support campaign funds.

Staff Play an Active Role in the Annual Campaign

How many staff members are involved with your organization? Full time? Part time? This is a powerful group of individuals that can play an influential role in your annual support campaign. Staff members know the value of the work that your organization is doing and also see the results of the efforts on a daily basis. They understand why and how your organization does the work it does. Staff are often among the most passionately committed individuals involved with your nonprofit. Make sure to engage them in the campaign well, make it enjoyable and educational, and reward them as appropriate for jobs well done.

Take the total number of full-time staff members making a gift and divide it by the number of total full-time staff members serving your organization. This will give you the percentage of full-time staff members making a charitable gift.

What percentage of your full-time staff members gives an annual support campaign gift?

Part-time Staff

While full-time staff members are definitely a vital part of your nonprofit, your part-time individuals also bring talents and treasures to your nonprofit organization. Part-time staff members sometimes are even more enthusiastic, as they do not get caught up in the daily grind that so many full-time staff members do. Certainly there are diverse reasons why people work part time, but they may bring with them a fresh perspective, a less-encumbered vibrancy, and their own levels of relationship and commitment. Do not underestimate or take for granted any individual associated with your organization. Each of them can bring skills and appropriate gifts to the organization.

Take the total number of part-time staff members making a gift and divide it by the number of total part-time staff members serving your organization. This will give you the percentage of part-time staff members making a charitable gift.

What percentage of your part-time staff members gives an annual support campaign gift?

Staff Members Supporting Annual Support Campaign Work in Their Job Description

Many nonprofit organizations believe that if someone is working on fundraising and philanthropy in general, it is that person's job to make the money happen. If your nonprofit holds this philosophy, it is something you will have to work to change over time, if you are ever to achieve all that you can in your annual support campaign. When all people in a nonprofit organization understand that they have a role to play in charitable support, you are another huge step toward having a high-functioning annual support campaign. In an ideal world, this is where you are or are heading toward.

How many of your staff members are actively engaged in support of annual support campaign work? How many have, as part of their job description, some role in annual support campaign work?

Take the total number of staff members with annual support work of some sort and divide it by the number of total staff members serving your organization. This will give you the percentage of staff members who have, at least as part of their job, to support the annual campaign through their job efforts.

What percentage of your staff members has an active and specific, defined role in the annual support campaign, as outlined in their job description?

Everyone should have some role in supporting the annual support campaign.

Major Gifts

Before we begin to outline the major gifts teams and how we will plan for their success, it is helpful to have some understanding of what a major gift is at your organization. When I work as a consultant with nonprofit organizations, one of the first things I typically do is to look at their current gifts and understand their current donor base and where it stands.

At many organizations, a major gift is described as a $1,200 gift or more, as it represents a $100 per month pledge over the course of one year.

To determine what a major gift is at your nonprofit organization, run a report of the entire amount of annual support gifts that you received last year. Then take the top 10% of those gifts. For the purposes of this exercise, we will call them major gifts.

How many annual support campaign gifts were given to your organization last year?

Take the top 10% of the total number of gifts given. For example, if you had 500 gifts to annual support last year, this would mean to take the 50 largest gifts to annual support and look at their amounts from smallest to largest.

What is the smallest gift in this segment?

What is the largest gift amount given in this segment?

Both of these amounts represent major gifts to your organization, and it is important to understand this segment so that we can figure out how to get more of these types of gifts. In my experience, in a high-functioning annual support campaign, up to 60% of the overall annual support campaign goal for a given year will come from the top 10% of donors. This makes planning for, and spending time on, this significant base a critical part of your campaign success.

Volunteers Actively Involved in Major Gift Fundraising for the Annual Campaign

When calculating how many volunteers are involved in an annual support campaign, clients I work with often want to include volunteers who are helping them with specific special events and other functions as individuals who are helping in the annual support campaign major gifts division. While this is tempting and can help make your numbers look larger, it is best to differentiate, for planning purposes, annual support campaign volunteers and special events or other volunteers. If we are to have our highest-functioning fundraising and our most effective annual support campaign, we must make sure that our fundraising volunteers are accounted for appropriately at every level. By doing this, we help to ensure that we will have our best result possible each and every year.

Look at the total number of annual support campaign volunteers in the past year who were involved in major gifts; focus specifically on gifts that are in the top 10% of gifts to your organization.

How many major gifts volunteers did you have in this year's annual support campaign?

How many returning major gifts volunteers did you have in your annual support campaign?

How many new major gifts volunteers did you have in your annual support campaign?

How many of those major gifts volunteers gave a gift to your annual support campaign?

How many of those major gifts volunteers gave a gift and got a gift for your annual support campaign?

Gifts and Pledges

Total Gifts and Pledges

What is the total number of gifts to your annual support campaign? When your total gift number is growing, it means that you are communicating your mission and goals to a large number of people and that they are hearing your message well enough to make a charitable gift. If your gift number is declining, you need to understand why so that you can determine how to change that as appropriate. A rising gift number may or may not mean rising gift revenue, but it does likely mean that you are telling your story to more people. In most cases, that is a very good thing.

Number of New Gifts and Pledges

New gifts mean new people who are convinced enough about your organization to make a gift or at least who have been motivated to make a gift. This means that something you are doing this year is better than what you were doing last year. While this may seem simple, understanding what works well in fundraising and what does not is a worthwhile endeavor. When you can look back on a campaign and determine why you have raised more money and have more new money in hand than in previous years, you can identify people and behaviors that can be encouraged and repeated in years to come. This is one of the best ways that we learn in our industry—by seeing what has worked well and replicating it over and over until we learn something better. New gifts are a sure sign that something has worked well, and you likely need to figure out a way to do more of it.

Research shows that certain gifts may cost more money than they bring in, but it is important to remember that an annual support campaign is about more than just the money. It is also about raising awareness, making friends, and telling the story of the admirable work that you are doing in the community. If handled well, this year's less-than-cost-effect gifts will likely increase over the years. Who knows who will become your next major gift donor? Cultivating donors and their gifts is a bit like gardening: Plant the seeds, provide the necessities, and with a little attention over the years, they will flourish to be a lovely bounty for you for years to come.

Number of New Major Gifts and Pledges

One facet of your annual support campaign that will fuel your new growth is the number of new major gifts that are added each year to your effort. This may include an upgrade of someone from a $100 gift to a $1,000 gift, or it may include someone coming into your campaign efforts as a $5,000 contributor. Both would be considered as "new" major gifts. By tracking and being intentional about the identification, solicitation, and growth of this segment of your annual support campaign, you are helping to ensure that the 60% of your campaign goal that is often made up of this segment, continues to grow and mature.

Another reason to make sure that you focus heavily on this segment of donors is the possibility and probability that your *next* big campaign will be fueled by these same individuals, corporations, and foundations. By making sure that you grow and develop this group, you are ensuring that future campaigns have the basis that they will need for success. Whether these campaigns end up being annual, capital, or endowment is for the future to determine. When you build annual support campaign major gifts each year, however, you are helping to make sure that future campaigns are formed as well. By focusing on this sector, you are developing for the future.

Donor Retention Rate for Major Gifts and Pledges

If you have had an annual campaign effort before in some form, you will have existing major gifts from previous years. How many of those gifts did you get back in this year's campaign? This is a good area to focus on in campaign planning for your upcoming annual support campaign. You will want to be sure to have plans to get to know, thank, and steward all of your various donors as appropriate, but you will want to make especially sure that your major donors feel and know that they are appreciated. If you do not have good retention of your annual support campaign major gifts segment, you will have an almost impossible struggle to grow your campaign over time. You will just get gifts in the front door and have them leave out the back door. This is no way to grow your financial development program. Investing resources to cultivate, maintain, and retain these donors is a key aspect of your current and future campaign success.

Donor Retention Rate of All Gifts Other Than Major Gifts and Pledges

You should track and measure the retention rate of all gifts outside of major gifts as well to see how you are doing, whom you are missing, and how you can improve and engage this group better. Donors inherently have value to your organization and we are well served to try to retain donors and their gifts. Look at who gave to your campaign last year and then compare it with everyone who gave this year. What is your retention rate? Why do you think the donors who did not give this year did not make a gift? Understanding these dynamics as well as your return rate for donors and pledges will take you a long way towards having a better and stronger fundraising effort this year. If the reasons that your donors are leaving is something that you can and should be controlling, then you know you have work to do. If your donors are leaving for reasons outside of your control (moving away, having financial problems, etc.) then you know that you are doing the best that you can with the resources that you have.

Collecting the Gifts

Collection Rate of Gift/Pledges

Gifts are good only if they are collected. This may seem simple in concept, but I have worked with many campaigns that focused very hard on the getting of annual support campaign pledges, then gave little or no focus to campaign collections.

The highest collection rate that I have ever been involved with in an annual support campaign is one of a 96% collection rate. This means that in a $100,000 annual support campaign, $96,000 would actually come in the door at the end of the effort. This percentage can vary depending on the campaign, but the more that you encourage campaign pledging, the more you risk having a lower collection rate. Pledges may greatly raise your average gift size, but remember that pledges are merely promises that you must make the effort to actually obtain. You should track and understand your collection rate of pledges and gifts so that you can work to improve and enhance your efforts each and every year. Remember that money that is pledged but never given does not help your campaign or the mission of your organization. It results in wasted effort and broken promises—neither of which we want to encourage.

Most Effective Means of Collection/Payment

By recognizing how people pay and you collect, you can better understand what is working for your annual support campaign collection efforts and what is not. Again, while this may seem simple on the surface, understanding how people pay you can affect how you decide to take and receive payments in future years. When people pay by credit card, there is only a very small failure rate compared to when they send a check through the mail, where there is a much higher nonpayer rate. Understanding this might help you to develop new and better payment plans based on a monthly debit from a credit card, for example. I can almost guarantee that your particular organizational payment plan policy will develop over a period of years. By working closely with your finance team, you can help to make the best payment plan policies for your organization. Here are a few things to remember about payments:

- The more immediate, the better. However you receive the pledge, the quicker donors can take action toward paying the pledge, the better.
- The simpler, the better. The easier it is for the donor, the more likely it will happen quickly.

- The more spontaneous the ability to make payment, the better. By this I mean that if a person decides to give you $1 million in stock this afternoon, you can accept it this afternoon. Having systems in place that allow you to say yes to accepting their payment helps to raise the likelihood that any payment will happen. This is true whether it is a cell phone payment charge coming to your organization or a large stock transaction.

Remember, if you allow for time to pass between the pledge commitment and the payment of the gift, both passion and commitment for the making of the gift can dwindle. When this happens, your opportunity to receive the gift may change as well.

Accuracy of Campaign Information

Information from pledge cards and other materials is very useful for this campaign and for any future fundraising efforts. It is important to manage this information conscientiously and with the utmost of care for three reasons.

1. There is the issue of security surrounding having credit card numbers, checks, and other personal information from your donors. Certainly you do not want to have a breach in that operation.

2. You want to capture all the possible information from the pledge cards, and do it accurately. Few things are more frustrating for campaign volunteers than wrong numbers and bad addresses. When people are giving their time, they want it to be used as well as possible.

3. With a large campaign, the number of pledge cards can be substantial, so the administrator will need a good system in place, or a good beginning, reworked as necessary.

No database is perfect, but you want to be sure that you have the best information possible for your campaign efforts. By having a highly capable person whose job it is to process and manage campaign information, you help to guarantee that your information will be accurate and complete. As I stated earlier, I would rather have a great person managing my information than to have the latest or greatest fundraising software. If you are not taking your campaign information seriously and processing it to the absolute best of your abilities, you are jeopardizing your current campaign as well as any future campaign efforts.

Setting the Money Goal

I have intentionally left this as one of the last topics in the text as it is often "the money" that people first think of when they think of the annual support campaign. While it is important and critical to organizational success, hopefully you have seen from this text that it is not the first or only thing to consider when planning your annual support campaign. As you can see from the Annual Support Campaign Evaluation Tool shown on page 267, there are many ways to measure success in an annual support campaign outside of the actual money raised. Make sure to celebrate your successes, both monetary and otherwise, with your staff and volunteers.

Setting the money goal for your annual support campaign is part art and part science. If it is your first year doing annual support, I strongly encourage you to look at setting a goal that is both highly achievable and strong for morale. If you do not succeed your first year, it is much more likely that you will not have another annual support campaign. This would lead to a less-than-positive long-term result as you likely return to poor fundraising habits and performance.

If it is your second year doing annual support or later, then you likely have some idea of what your capabilities were, operating under your last year's paradigm. This is important because it is hoped that with the new knowledge contained in this text, you can greatly advance your campaign compared with last year. Let us look at some ideas around goal setting and see if they can help you understand the art and science of setting campaign goals.

If it is your first year doing annual support, set a goal that is obtainable and achievable while still making headway toward your long-term goals and objectives. For many, this means setting a goal that is likely lower than top leadership would like to raise, but slightly higher than a nervous development director might want to have as a campaign goal. My feeling is that you absolutely should be able to hit your first campaign goal. It builds morale, positive feelings around the campaign concept, and volunteer and staff success. All of these emotions are priceless when it comes to forming good habits and moving toward next year's campaign success as well. Consider a campaign scenario where the first-year goal is to raise $50,000. Staff and volunteers work hard and the campaign raises $60,000. Yeah! We beat our goal by $10,000! It feels pretty good, right?

Well, let us imagine the same campaign with a campaign goal of $100,000. Staff and volunteers work hard and raise $60,000. Ugh! It does not feel as good, does it? No. We want our staff and volunteers—especially when we are embracing a new strategy or concept—to have and feel success so that the positive behaviors that have been created are replicated and continued for years to come. In the first year, set your annual support campaign goal so that you are highly confident that you can achieve it. It will help you build positive momentum for years to come.

Let us look now at how you might address a second-year campaign goal. A simple rule of thumb is to set your campaign goal at what you raised last year and build a plan to surpass it. If it was the second year in the earlier example and last year you raised $60,000, you would likely look at setting your campaign goal at around $60,000 or somewhat higher, depending on your confidence level and organizational strengths. Again, use good judgment in setting your external campaign goals. You want to have your staff and volunteers feel successful, and it is also positive for your community to feel that the organization is meeting its objectives as well. How you communicate your success or failure regarding annual support can affect future fundraising, board recruitment, and other organizational efforts. By setting attainable campaign goals, you set your organization up to have a feeling of success.

Note that in the last paragraph, I mentioned the idea of "external" campaign goals. Your organization can have both internal and external campaign goals. An external campaign goal might be $60,000 while an internal campaign goal might be $75,000. All plans and teams are built so that your organization has a strong opportunity to raise $75,000 but the lay volunteers and community understand the goal to be $60,000. This is just one way of managing goals and objectives while keeping volunteer and community morale in mind. We want to meet our organizational goals and objectives, but we also want our volunteers to feel great about the important work that they are doing in their community. Remember, if they reach the $75,000, they will feel tremendous about their overachieving.

Evaluating

Evaluation is a valuable exercise in the annual support campaign. Taking the time to reflect on past performance allows everyone the opportunity to note jobs well done as well as places for improvement. No matter what year of annual support campaign you are embarking on, there is always room for enhancement. Especially with annual support campaigns, each year is another opportunity to learn and grow. Exhibit 8.1 is designed for you to compile the information from your last year's campaign or keep track of this year's

---

EXHIBIT 8.1

Annual Campaign Evaluation Tool

Staff	Last Year	This Year	Next Year
# of Full-time (FT) Staff Supporting Campaign Volunteers			
Comments/Suggestions for Improving:			
# of Part-time (PT) Staff Supporting Campaign Volunteers			
Comments/Suggestions for Improving:			
Percentage of FT Staff Donating to the Campaign			
Comments/Suggestions for Improving:			
Percentage of PT Staff Donating to the Campaign			
Comments/Suggestions for Improving:			
# of FT Staff Involved in Campaign Planning and Implementation			
Comments/Suggestions for Improving:			
# of PT Staff Involved in Campaign Planning and Implementation			
Comments/Suggestions for Improving:			

(continued)

Board	Last Year	This Year	Next Year
Total # of Board Members			
Comments/Suggestions for Improving:			
Percentage of Board members Donating to the Campaign			
Comments/Suggestions for Improving:			
Percentage of Board Members Making a Gift in the Top 10% of Gifts to the Campaign			
Comments/Suggestions for Improving:			
Percentage of Board Members Participating as Campaigners (giving own gift and getting at least one more)			
Comments/Suggestions for Improving:			
Number of Board Members Taking a Leadership Role in the Annual Support Campaign			
Comments/Suggestions for Improving:			

Major Gifts Teams	Last Year	This Year	Next Year
# of Individuals Returning as Campaigners from Last Year			
Comments/Suggestions for Improving:			
# of New Individuals Serving as Campaigners			
Comments/Suggestions for Improving:			
# of Campaigners Participating in Training			
Comments/Suggestions for Improving:			
# of Campaigners Donating Their Own Gift Prior to Start of Campaign			
Comments/Suggestions for Improving:			
# of Campaigners Giving Own Gift and Getting at Least One Other			

(continued)

EXHIBIT 8.1 (*Continued*)

Comments/Suggestions for Improving:

# of Campaigners Achieving Indvidual Campaign Goal

Comments/Suggestions for Improving:

Community Gifts Teams	Last Year	This Year	Next Year
# of Individuals Returning as Campaigners from Last Year			
Comments/Suggestions for Improving:			
# of New Individuals Serving as Campaigners			
Comments/Suggestions for Improving:			
# of Campaigners Participating in Training			
Comments/Suggestions for Improving:			
# of Campaigners Donating Their Own Gift Prior to Start of Campaign			
Comments/Suggestions for Improving:			
# of Campaigners Giving Own Gift and Getting at Least One Other			
Comments/Suggestions for Improving:			
# of Campaigners Achieving Indvidual Campaign Goal			
Comments/Suggestions for Improving:			

Donor Engagement	Last Year	This Year	Next Year
Total # of Gifts to the Annual Support Campaign			
Comments/Suggestions for Improving:			
Total # of New Gifts to the Annual Support Campaign			
Comments/Suggestions for Improving:			
Total # of Renewed Gifts to the Annual Support Campaign			
Comments/Suggestions for Improving:			
Number of New Major Gifts (Top 10% of Overall Gifts) to the Annual Support Campaign			

(*continued*)

Comments/Suggestions for Improving:

Number of Renewed Major Gifts (Top 10% of Overall Gifts) to the Annual Support Campaign

Comments/Suggestions for Improving:

Overall Collection Rate at End of Campaign

Comments/Suggestions for Improving:

Overall Collection Rate at End of 12 Months Following Campaign Ending Date

Comments/Suggestions for Improving:

Subjective Planning and Evaluation Information

Rank on a Scale of 1–10 with 10 Being Outstanding	**Last Year**	**This Year**	**Next Year**
Campaign Planning Process			
Comments/Suggestions for Improving:			
Calendar of Annual Support Campaign			
Comments/Suggestions for Improving:			
Communication of Overall Campaign to Staff			
Comments/Suggestions for Improving:			
Communication of Overall Campaign to Volunteers			
Comments/Suggestions for Improving:			
Communication of Overall Campaign to Donors			
Comments/Suggestions for Improving:			
Communication of Overall Campaign to Our Own Constituency			
Comments/Suggestions for Improving:			
Communication of Overall Campaign to the Overall Community			
Comments/Suggestions for Improving:			
Process of Recruiting Campaigners			
Comments/Suggestions for Improving:			
Solicitation Practices Done by Staff			

(continued)

EXHIBIT 8.1 (*Continued*)

Comments/Suggestions for Improving:

Solicitation Practices Performed by Volunteers

Comments/Suggestions for Improving:

Explanation and Understanding of Job
Descriptions

Comments/Suggestions for Improving:

Campaign Meetings and Agendas

Comments/Suggestions for Improving:

Campaign Follow Up and Follow Through

Comments/Suggestions for Improving:

Campaign Collection Processes

Comments/Suggestions for Improving:

Donor Acknowledgement Process

Comments/Suggestions for Improving:

Donor Recognition Process

Comments/Suggestions for Improving:

Donor Thanking Process

Comments/Suggestions for Improving:

Overall Attitude of Staff towards Annual
Support Campaign

Comments/Suggestions for Improving:

Overall Attitude of Board towards Annual
Support Campaign

Comments/Suggestions for Improving:

Overall Attitude of Campaign Volunteers
toward Annual Support Campaign

Comments/Suggestions for Improving:

General Spirit of the Annual Support Campaign

Comments/Suggestions for Improving:

Other?

Comments/Suggestions for Improving:

information to be used as a basis for next year. Taking the time for assessment and record keeping will allow you to quickly determine where to focus extra attention in the future. Build on your success and learn from your failures.

Now that you have seen the various issues that might concern your annual support campaign, you can take the information that you learned in this chapter to build an annual support campaign plan for your nonprofit organization.

Volunteer's Evaluation

Volunteers are such a fundamental part of your annual support campaign efforts, it is best to understand their hopes, concerns, and thoughts on the campaign and how it went. At campaign victory celebrations when you bring all of the campaign volunteers together to thank and recognize their achievements, have them fill out a short survey about their campaign experience. Send it to anyone who was not able to attend the event for any reason. A copy of one evaluation that I have used follows.

Exercise

Annual Support Campaign Evaluation Tool

Please rate the following from 1 to 4 (1 being unacceptable and 4 being exceptional):

1. Communication with your team
   1 2 3 4
2. Amount of communication from the nonprofit
   1 2 3 4
3. Training and preparation that you received from the nonprofit
   1 2 3 4
4. Printed materials and support documents
   1 2 3 4
5. Meeting formats
   1 2 3 4

---

6. Length of meetings

    1 2 3 4

7. Did you get the assistance or support you needed from staff?

    1 2 3 4

8. Did you have fun during the campaign?

    1 2 3 4

9. Will you give your time next year to the campaign?

    1 2 3 4

10. How many years have you worked with the campaign?

    1 2 3 4 More (Write Number)

_____

11. What part of the campaign did you like best?

_____

_____

_____

12. What part of the campaign did you like least?

_____

_____

_____

13. What ideas do you have to make the campaign better?

_____

_____

_____

14. Other comments:

_____

_____

Optional: Name:

Phone: _____

Email: _____

An evaluation like this one gives your volunteers a chance to provide feedback on what worked and what did not work in your annual support campaign. Slightly altering the evaluation would give you a document to hand out to your staff as well. Add or delete things through the years, as appropriate, to gain the best insight. A strong evaluation process can help you get better every year, identifying and carefully addressing problem areas and collaborating on ideas for improvements. When you get an evaluation with challenges, work hard to deal with them as quickly as possible. Staff members and volunteers are two of your most important resources. By managing their concerns with sincerity and integrity, you will go far in retaining and gaining high performance from them in the short and the long run.

Summary

It is imperative to your success that you decide on goals and objectives first and have as much agreement among decision makers as possible. A strong annual campaign starts with an honest assessment of where your organization is currently, or how last year's annual campaign really went. The next vital piece of the annual campaign is a solid plan that gives your teams the direction they need to accomplish this great work. Then you must plan carefully, so that the roads you take lead you to your chosen destination. By looking ahead to build the best campaign possible, you are helping to make sure that you raise the most money while telling the inspiring stories about your organization in the community. A well run campaign is active in creating the reality you want, rather than settling for less than is possible.

After all the enthusiasm of the campaign and the excitement of the events are over, take the time to debrief with your staff and volunteers before the specifics are forgotten. There is much to be gained immediately following a venture; the details are fresh, and the ideas for improvements will flow more easily. A good campaign finishes with a thorough evaluation of what went right and what went wrong. The best thing about an annual campaign is that it happens every year. You get to try again next year and improve your performance. By having a thorough evaluation that measures what happened as well as what did not happen, you help to make next year's campaign even better. Each year your annual campaign will undoubtedly run smoother. You will have more systems in place, you will know what is coming rather than reacting, and you will mold your campaign to best utilize your community resources to advance your good work. Take the time to evaluate what has happened; that will turn into your plan for next year.

Understand the dynamics associated with a year round annual campaign program and you will have a viable campaign that will serve your organization well this year and lay the foundation for next year and future years as well. Remember to focus on key measurements before, during and after your annual campaign that include volunteer recruitment and engagement. And also, learn from your annual campaign successes and your failures and get better every year!

You CAN run a super annual campaign with the involvement of staff and volunteers; you owe it to yourself, your organization, and your community.

Index

J

Jerry Lewis Labor Day Muscular
Dystrophy Telethon, 15
job descriptions
campaign chair's, 146–47 exhibit
5.2
campaign division chair's, 147–48
exhibit 5.2
campaigner's, 149–50 exhibit 5.2
campaign team leader's, 148–49
exhibit 5.2
volunteer gift giving, 145

L

large gifts, 39
asking for, 47–48, 249
benefit of cultivation efforts, 202
as campaign goal, 176
how used, 62
influential volunteers and, 201
reasons for, 78
reluctance to give, 195
wealthy people and, 141–42
leaders
community, 131
developing and training, 36–37
organizational, 130–31
leadership
campaign, 167–72
developing and practicing, 126–27
discovering, 32–33
management skills and staff, 52–53

volunteer experience, 52
Lions Club, 33
local media, 8
local newspaper, 9
long-term
employees, 170
funding, 3
fundraising program, 17
goals, 26
importance, 119
performance objectives, 71
relationships, 78
sustainability, 12, 135
volunteers, 78

M

making a difference, 126
mass media, 15
MasterCard, 13
mission
funding your, 30
of organization, 126
oriented work, 20, 56
statement, 60, 86, 98

N

networking, 8, 24, 39, 88, 127–28,
143
newsletter
advertising campaign, 12
announcements of gifts, 222
articles in, 46

tips and techniques, 214–15

visit, follow-up after the, 221–23

retention rate, 256–57

Rotary Club, 33

S

sales ventures, 13–14

senior managers, 140–41

special events

about, 5–11

prospect lists, 8–9

ten reasons for, 6

things to do afterwards, 9–10

things to think about, 7

spirit factor, 245–47

staff

annual campaign and, 251

campaign building, 171–73, 172
exhibits 6.2–6.3

campaign information managing, 79–80

component, 169–71, 173

job description of, 252

keys to hiring great, 26–28

leadership and management skills, 52–53

members, 22–23, 25, 89

need to be friendly, 25–26

part-time, 251

responsibilities, 23

success, keys to, 24–25

State Employees Campaign, 11

steward(s)

"can you steward gifts appropriately?", 81–82

of charitable funds, 28, 50, 55, 63, 78

of funds raised, 22

organizations that are good, 21

stewardship

of current donors, 26, 256

as donor cultivation, 32

practices in annual campaign, 46

stories illustrating passion, 106

story tellers, 32

strategic plan of organization, 60–61

support case

about, 93–94

annual support, developing case of, 94

campaign, how it will change the world, 98–99

campaign brochure, 95–96

changes achieved, 103

community funding benefits, 102

community issues, 94–95, 97–99

exercise: benefits of community funding, 102

exercise: community involvement by organization, 97

exercise: community support from campaign, 98

exercise: high impact changes achieved, 103